THE RANGERS STORY

AN OFFICIAL HISTORY OF RANGERS FOOTBALL CLUB

Douglas Russell

g

Grange
Lomond Books

© 1998
Published by Grange Communications Ltd., Edinburgh,
under licence from The Rangers Football Club plc.

Printed in the UK

ISBN 0 947782 01 X

Contents

INTRODUCTION

RANGERS FOOTBALL CLUB is a unique institution, part of the very fabric and tradition of Scottish life. Among the country's oldest and by far its most successful club, Rangers has grown from humble beginnings as a virtual youth club in Victorian Glasgow into the football colossus it is today. Touched occasionally by the cruel hand of fate, tragedy has merely intensified the remarkable solidarity of a staunch support.

It all began with four youths back in February 1872. Brothers Peter and Moses McNeil, Peter Campbell and William McBeath decided to form their own football team whilst out walking in West End Park (Kelvinbridge), Glasgow. The name *'Rangers'* came from an English rugby team known to Moses.

The earliest matches were played on the public pitches of Fleshers' Haugh on Glasgow Green until a home ground was secured at Burnbank three years later. The following year saw a switch to the south side, to Kinning Park, which remained Rangers' home until the move, in August 1887, to the Ibrox area of Glasgow, the club rightly judging the westward spread of the city's growing population. In those far-off days, Ibrox was considered *"out in the country"*.

The site of old Ibrox Park was adjacent to the current stadium but on the other side of Copland Road. Rangers finally made the short move to their present home in December 1899.

Nothing more powerfully depicts the present stature of the club than the magnificence of the redeveloped stadium, originally built in response to the ever-increasing growth in popularity of the sport and to reflect Rangers' increasingly dominant position in Scottish football. Central to the development of Ibrox Stadium was the construction of the Grandstand (today's Main Stand), officially opened on New Year's Day, 1929. The "New Ibrox" was instigated by the foresight of Willie Waddell in the wake of the disaster of 1971 and was given fresh impetus by modern safety legislation and the challenge of meeting the demanding standards of European competition.

The history of Rangers is well documented. This volume is intended as a supplement to the various versions of that glorious tale, highlighting some of the occasions and personalities that have lit up these past 125 years.

Names like Waddell, Baxter, Greig, Cooper, Hateley and Gascoigne are music to the ears of any *'True Blue'*. Read about them here and marvel at their feats.

Recall the days when Rangers strode the Scottish stage like a colossus, from the thirties, through the sixties and into the nineties. If your heart warms to the sound of the above names and skips a beat at the very mention of Ibrox stadium, you will find much to savour between these covers.

RANGERS V. CELTIC

BELIEVE IT OR NOT, Rangers actually lost the first-ever encounter between the teams by five goals to two! This was prior to the formation of the Scottish League in 1890. Eventually, the 'Light Blues' would claim the scalp of the team from the East End of the city in the Glasgow Cup Final of season 1892/93, the 3-1 scoreline also ensuring that Rangers lifted this trophy for the first time.

The following year, and another first, as the rivals met again in the final of the Scottish Cup. Although Celtic were the current champions, Rangers had crushed them 5-0 in a league encounter before this game. The team in blue triumphed 3-1 as the Scottish Cup was won for the first time since the formation of the club in 1872.

Celtic would then dominate, with victories in the Scottish Cup Final of season 1898/99 (thus depriving Rangers of their first-ever league and cup 'double') and the semi final the following year (4-0 after a 2-2 drawn game). The next time Rangers won this trophy (in season 1902/03) the Parkhead club were beaten 3-0 at the quarter-final stage.

In 1905, the 'Light Blues' lost the League Championship to the 'Bhoys' after a play-off but for real high drama, fast forward to the Scottish Cup Final of 1909 and the infamous *"Day They Burned Down Hampden"*.

Following a 2-2 draw, the replay also ended all square - at 1-1. Both sets of fans demanded extra time as a rumour was circulating that cup-ties were deliberately being drawn, thus ensuring extra gate receipts for the clubs! Hundreds of fans invaded the Hampden pitch and a number of 'pay-boxes' were set alight. Many policemen and supporters were injured in the ensuing riot before order was restored some two-and-a-half hours later. After consultation with both Rangers and Celtic, the game was officially abandoned by the Football Association and the trophy withheld. The following month, however, there was cause for celebration when Celtic were beaten 4-2 in the Charity Cup Final.

Season 1910/11 and Rangers were rewarded with their sixth Championship, their first since 1902. Due to ground work at Ibrox, both 'home' and 'away' games were played at Parkhead, resulting in a 1-1 draw and 1-0 victory to the 'Light Blues'.

After the notorious Scottish Cup Final of 1909, it would be several years (season 1919/20) before the 'Old Firm' would face up to each other again in this competition. A 1-0 victory at the quarter-final stage was really just the blue icing on a blue cake of a year in which Rangers reigned supreme - the Championship was taken with only two defeats in a total of forty-two games. The following year and another league title, with Celtic ten points behind in second place.

The Scottish Cup jinx continued to haunt Rangers, however, as Celtic were convincing winners (5-0) in the semi final of 1925. It seemed that many at Ibrox had, indeed, forgotten what this trophy looked like, as it had never been seen inside the Stadium since last won in 1903! All that would change, at last, on a spring day in 1928 ....

That year's Cup Final was between the current League Champions (Rangers) and the Scottish Cup holders (Celtic). In truth, the first 'forty-five' was all Celtic, with Tom Hamiton performing wonders in the Rangers goal (shades of Andy Goram) to keep the score 0-0 at the interval. The second half was a different proposition. Captain Davie Meiklejohn's penalty goal was followed by strikes from Bob McPhail and Sandy Archibald (2) to secure one of the famous victories in front of a record 118,115 crowd. The twenty-five year hoodoo was well and truly smashed! Surprisingly, the sides would not clash again in this particular competition until season 1952/53.

Tragedy struck when the teams locked horns on league business in September 1931. Celtic goalkeeper, John Thomson, had been injured following an accidental clash with Rangers forward Sam English and, sadly, died. It was a powerful reminder that, despite the great rivalry, at the end of the day, it really was only a game.

From the end of the 'Great War' (1914-18) to the commencement of hostilities at the start of the Second World War (1939-45), the Ibrox club had accumulated a total of fifteen titles as opposed to Celtic's five, with both teams lifting the Scottish Cup on six occasions.

In the first post-war season of 1946-47, the 'Light Blues' won the Charity Cup, beating Celtic 1-0 in the final. The feat was repeated the following year but this time with a 2-0 scoreline. Records fell by the wayside in 1949, when Rangers became the first Scottish team to secure the 'treble' of League Flag, Scottish and League Cups. The side had struggled early on that year in the League Cup and, in fact, only qualified from their section by beating Celtic 2-1 (in the last game) in front of a quite astonishing crowd of 105,000 supporters.

The 'Eastenders' were beaten 4-0 at Ibrox on the road to further Championship glory in the title race of 1949/50 and, one year on, lost 2-1 in the early stages of the Charity Cup. This was the only piece of silverware garnished with blue ribbons that season.

The record books show that Rangers' first barren time since the end of the war was the period 1951/52. Yet, even then, not only had they defeated their greatest rivals 3-0 in the October semi final of the League Cup but also triumphed 4-1 in the traditional 'Ne'erday' fixture. Although the following year was another glorious 'double' for the club, league victories were shared one apiece, with each side winning their 'home' encounter. Also, for the first time since back in 1928, the clubs were paired together in the Scottish Cup (on this occasion in the quarter finals) before Rangers ran out 2-0 victors.

Celtic secured the title in season 1953/54, with the 'Light Blues' nine points behind in fourth position. Although neither of the rivals topped the table next time round, at least the 'Boys in Blue' had the satisfaction of a 4-1 New Year's Day conquest, with Johnny Hubbard scoring a 'hat-trick'. The little South African (5' 4" in height and less than 9 stones in weight) was the undisputed penalty king of his era. In his ten years at Ibrox, the 'Wee Man' converted an amazing fifty-four out of a possible fifty-seven spot kicks and, indeed, from 1949 to January 1956, scored with twenty-three successive attempts and, yes, one of his goals that day against Celtic was a penalty!

Although the Govan team were crowned Champions in 1956 (with the aforementioned Johnny Hubbard top goalscorer with thirty-three strikes), results between the 'Old Firm' balanced out during the season. For example, a 4-1 Celtic victory at Ibrox in the League Cup was followed four days later by a 4-0 Rangers triumph at Parkhead in the same competition. The title was retained in 1957 (with convincing 2-0 results both 'home' and 'away' against Celtic) but it was the 'Hoops' who ended our club's participation in both the League and Scottish Cups. The 'Light Blues' had come back from the dead in the Scottish Cup tie at Parkhead, scoring two late goals to draw the game 4-4 but it was all to no avail, as the replay was lost 2-0.

Season 1957/58 is chiefly remembered for a particularly 'Bad Day at Black Rock' when Rangers were put to the sword in the October League Cup Final. Few have forgotten the 7-1 scoreline. In the aftermath of this game, thirty-two-year-old Willie Telfer joined from St. Mirren to solidify the watery defence. Though viewed as a panic measure, it actually worked and the 'Blue Boys' were unbeaten in their next twenty league encounters. The great rivals met again, as per usual, on January 1st (at Parkhead) but this time, thankfully, the outcome was rather different and Alex Scott's solitary goal of the game captured the points for Rangers.

In Championship terms, Celtic were now lost in the wilderness (and would be for several years yet) but, in the strangest of circumstances, they played their part to perfection in 1959 and Rangers' 31st Flag. On the last day of that particular campaign, relegation-threatened Aberdeen visited Ibrox and Hearts (lying in second place) travelled to Parkhead. Victory for Rangers and the title was all theirs once again. It seemed relatively straightforward but, of course, this is not always the case on match days.

As if to prove a point, Aberdeen won 2-1 and avoided the 'drop'. The trophy would, therefore, reside at Gorgie Road for a year if the team from the capital could hold firm on their own date with destiny. Not for the last time, Hearts fell at the final hurdle and Celtic triumphed by two goals to one. One wonders what the outcome might have been today, in similar circumstances, with blanket radio coverage and, no doubt, simultaneous broadcasts from both grounds but, as it was, Celtic had done Rangers a huge favour. By way of contrast, in the Scottish Cup, the 'Light Blues' were knocked out of the competition by their greatest rivals for the second time in three years.

As the austere decade that was the fifties drew to a close, Rangers could reflect on five League Championships as opposed to only one by Celtic, with both clubs having raised the Scottish Cup on two separate occasions during the ten-year period.

That old trophy would be acquired for the 15th time in 1960 with our team seeing off the 'Hoops' at the semi-final stage. Centre-forward, Jimmy Millar, had been a particularly painful thorn in Celtic's side that season and netted on both occasions when points were up for grabs (3-1 'home') and 1-0 'away' on New Year's Day. Nor did he disappoint at Hampden in April, on cup semi-final day, when a header from all of sixteen yards cancelled out an early Chalmers goal to ensure a replay. His work was not done, of course, and four days later, Millar scored twice in Rangers' impressive 4-1 victory.

Postscript: Kilmarnock were beaten by two goals to nil in the final. Just guess whose name was against both!

That summer's arrival of twenty-year-old Jim Baxter - arguably the most naturally gifted player to wear the colours - saw the team from Govan blossom from a good unit into a great one. Maximum points were taken from the 'Bhoys' (for the second year in a row) on the way to title No. 32, with the dazzling 5-1 demolition in Glasgow's East End, the highlight of the campaign. To this day, Rangers' record league win at that ground. Baxter, himself, had an astonishing record against Celtic (in the 1960-65 period) with only two defeats in total of eighteen games.

Neither side could gain any advantage in the 1961/62 period, with both encounters drawn but, the following May, the team's were worlds apart although sharing the same stretch of grass. That year's Scottish Cup Final (the first involving the 'Old Firm' for thirty-five years) had gone to a replay (after an initial 1-1 draw) and would be witnessed by a crowd of over 120,000 at Hampden.

Still recalled as one of the most one-sided finals ever, Rangers turned on the style with tormentor-in-chief, Jim Baxter, orchestrating from midfield. The 3-0 scoreline hardly conveyed 'Blue' superiority on the day and, with some twenty minutes still remaining, the green and white fans had seen enough and left for an early tea. Celtic's record of seventeen Scottish Cup triumphs had now been equalled by a Rangers team that stood tall with the very best of them.

It was only fitting that a 'triple crown' of the three major domestic honours

Ralph Brand scores against Celtic in the Scottish Cup Final Replay of 1963.

should follow in season 1963/64 - with that 'other' team put to the sword no less than five times in five meetings. Now that *is* dominance!

The foes came face to face in October 1964 for the League Cup Final, when Jim Forrest netted twice in a 2-1 victory, enabling Rangers to retain the trophy. Centre-forward Forrest was one of the most prolific strikers ever seen at Ibrox and, that season, established two post-war records, with 30 League goals and 57 strikes in total. In fact, it was one of the former that took the 'Light Blues' to success in the 'derby' encounter of 1st January. Considered to be partly responsible for the infamous Scottish Cup defeat at Berwick in January 1967, Jim Forrest was transferred almost immediately to Preston North End. This would prove to be a major error on the part of the club.

Season 1965/66 saw Celtic win their first title in twelve years under new manager, Jock Stein. Yet, the 'Gers began the campaign positively and did not lose a game until Christmas Day, when Dunfermline won 3-2 at Ibrox. Worse would follow a week later, with a 5-1 defeat at Parkhead. Although the teams met for the second year running in the League Cup Final, with another 2-1 scoreline, it was the 'Eastenders' turn to celebrate. All was not doom and gloom, however, and a certain Dane would soon become part of Ibrox folklore. Many years later, a more famous countryman of his would also wear the 'Blue' to even greater acclaim.

The Scottish Cup Final of 1966 required a replay after a goalless first match.

Change of shorts for McKinnon, Scottish Cup Final Replay v Celtic, 1966.

The following Wednesday, Danish defender Kai Johansen's thunderous twenty-five-yard rocket was the only goal that night and the fullback became an instant hero. The trophy had now been won a record nineteen times.

Some memories remain crystal clear even with the passing of time. A thought had crossed my mind, not during the game itself but later, in Glasgow's St Enoch Square, whilst waiting to welcome the players to their then traditional after-match meal at the hotel. Next morning was 'Higher' maths at school and revision was still incomplete! Disappointingly, no 'pass' certificate was received that summer but, somehow, memories of walking home to the Maryhill district of the city with 'Big Davie' and the others that night, now seem far more important after all these years.

Jimmy Millar ready to pounce, Scottish Cup Final, 1966.

With Celtic firing on all cylinders at home and abroad in season 1966/67, Rangers were without a trophy for the first time in fifteen years. Although reaching the final of the League Cup, and outplaying their opponents in green, a 1-0 defeat was still recorded. The following year, despite not losing a league match until the last day of the campaign and taking three out of a possible four points from the Parkhead side, the 'Light Blues' still finished behind their great rivals in the Championship.

It was a similar story by April 1969 when, even though Celtic were beaten 'home' and 'away' in the league, second place was still all that was on offer. Even more depressing, was a calamitous 4-0 defeat on Scottish Cup Final day, with Rangers behind as early as the second minute! The clubs met again in the same competition the following February but in the quarter final. Alex MacDonald was ordered off in a most controversial encounter that Celtic won 3-1, scoring two late goals.

The new decade was still in its infancy when, against all the odds, Rangers triumphed over Celtic in the League Cup Final of October 1970. The Ibrox side were just not fancied at all, even before it was confirmed that 'Captain Courageous', John Greig, would miss the game through injury. As it was, a famous headed goal by a sixteen-year-old boy named Johnstone made it a memorable day. In time, young Derek would become a great Ranger - in more than one position!

The 'Old Firm' would generate more headlines in early January 1971 but, this time, for the saddest of all reasons, as disaster struck Ibrox for the second time that century. At the end of the traditional encounter, steel barriers on Stairway 13 (the 'Rangers' end) gave way to devastating effect, resulting in the loss of sixty-six lives, with one hundred and forty-five injured in the crush. Everything else faded into insignificance that season, which ended with Celtic beating Rangers in the Scottish Cup Final replay.

Season 1971/72 could hardly have begun more abysmally, with three defeats at Celtic's hands during the August/September period. At home, it was still *their* time but, further afield, a blue light was beginning to flicker in Barcelona ....

The possibility of a Championship edged a little closer the next year but one point ensured that the trophy would still remain across the city. The 'Centenary' Scottish Cup Final was a different matter entirely, however, and 122,714 fans witnessed a classic encounter. Tom Forsyth's memorable 'strike' (from all of six inches after the ball rolled along the goal-line) secured victory by the odd goal in five.

As *'Nine-in-a-Row'* was being celebrated elsewhere in the late spring of 1974, the 'Light Blues' were left to ponder once again - surely things could only get better. And they did as season 1974/75 got underway. A vital 2-1 win at Parkhead in the third game of the Championship race (Rangers' first victory at this ground in six years) was just the tonic required by the 'Follow-Followers'. Yet when the rivals met again in early January, it was a somewhat similar scenario in the league - Celtic out in front (by two points). However, a convincing 3-0 'Light Blue' victory (with goals from Derek Johnstone, Tommy McLean and Derek Parlane) and the initiative had been seized. Maybe, at last, the tide had turned.

Some three months later, on 29th March, Easter Road was the venue when the title was finally clinched. Rangers required a point from second-placed Hibernian to end an eleven-year famine. Colin Stein's header in the 1-1 draw was enough and Celtic's long reign was over, with blue skies in Edinburgh. At the time, most pundits suggested that Celtic's run of successive Championships would never, of course, be achieved again by any other club and the record would stand unchallenged.

Oh, ye of little faith!

The League Championship, Scottish Cup and League Cup were all won in season 1975/76, with Celtic the losers at Hampden in October, when Alex MacDonald's headed goal began the festivities on League Cup Final day. In the league that year, Celtic led by three points prior to the 'Ne'erday' game, which was won by a solitary Derek Johnstone goal. Rangers would remain unbeaten until the end of the season.

From one extreme to the other and, the following year, it was to be a 'double' for our rivals. Although controversy surrounded the Scottish Cup Final and a highly debatable penalty award to Celtic, Lynch's conversion sealed the trophy's ultimate destination.

There can be no doubt that the arrival of Davie Cooper, Gordon Smith and Bobby Russell had an immediate effect after the huge disappointments of that barren period and season 1977/78 was covered in glory with the return of the three major domestic trophies to Govan. On the road to title No. 37, Celtic were beaten 3-2 and 3-1 in September and January respectively and, later on in March, were 2-1 extra-time victims in the League Cup Final, when Davie Cooper and Gordon Smith were on target.

Rangers really should have taken the crown again in May 1979, when a single point from the 'away' fixture in Glasgow's East End would have been enough. At 1-0 up, and with Celtic reduced to ten men, the 'Light Blues' unaccountably became cautious in the extreme, allowing the 'home' side the advantage. The record books confirm that Celtic won 4-2 and took the title. The rivals had also clashed earlier in the League Cup Semi Final, which the 'Gers won 3-2 on their way to retaining the trophy.

The wrong type of headlines would embarrass both clubs in the early summer of 1980 at Hampden, following a pitch invasion by supporters from each side of the divide. Before the trouble, an even final had gone to extra time and been decided in Celtic's favour by a deflected goal. Nonetheless, the abiding image that most folk recall is that of Strathclyde mounted police on the turf, endeavouring to take control. The old stadium had witnessed less volatile scenes the previous summer, when the Drybrough Cup had been lifted after a 3-1 triumph over Celtic with Davie Cooper's goal, in particular, fondly remembered.

With the advent of the eighties, fresh hope filled the minds of those who followed the 'Blue', thanks to double victories over their antagonists in the league (2-1, August 1980 and 3-0, November 1980). It was to prove a false dawn, however, with Rangers finishing twelve points behind them at season's end. The same total separated the clubs one year down the line.

The League Cup Final was lost to Celtic (2-1) in season 1982/83 but thankfully, there was, at least, a little light at the end of the tunnel in the final of the same competition twelve months on, when the teams came face to face yet again. A famous Ally McCoist 'hat-trick' cancelled out two replies and the silverware was back at Ibrox for a record 12th time.

Rangers failed to dominate Celtic in any of their four league encounters in season 1984/85 (with three of the games drawn), as both sides watched Aberdeen take the title. Next time round, there was little to choose between them, with one victory apiece and two drawn matches. Certainly the 4-4 drama at Ibrox had excitement aplenty and seemed to be one of those too few occasions when even neutrals applauded.

Less than one month after that eight-goal thriller, an announcement would be made to change forever, not only Rangers, but the face of Scottish football as well. Celtic would learn all about dominance from the other side of the coin - Graeme James Souness had joined the club as player-manager. At least the year ended on a high note, as the new man watched his charges record a 3-2 victory over Celtic in the Glasgow Cup Final, with another McCoist 'hat-trick'.

The new era began, to all intents and purposes at the start of season 1986/87. Although Rangers won the first league meeting (1-0), by late November their greatest rivals were nine points ahead in the race. Not for the first time, the 'Ne'erday' game would be absolutely crucial. As it was, on a miserable January day, thousands of blue revellers danced in the rain and snow, toasting a 2-0 result. But something else happened that day and it was all to do with the way victory had been achieved - Souness strode the sodden turf like a Colossus, encouraging his team to play with an arrogance and confidence not seen for a very long time. Celtic were beaten in more ways than one and, psychologically, had suffered a huge blow.

The Championship was finally clinched at Pittodrie in early May - for the first time in nine years - with Celtic six points behind. Already in place in the Ibrox trophy room was the League Cup, after a dramatic 2-1 showdown against Celtic, when a striker named Maurice Johnston was sent off!

Congratulations for Robert Fleck after his goal against Celtic, New Years Day, 1987.

The 'Old Firm' jousts had a major bearing on the destination of the following year's title. Celtic, having taken up the challenge, dropped only one point against the defending champions and would eventually cross the line twelve points ahead of the team from Govan. Rangers' solitary point was gained in the contentious 2-2 draw at Ibrox (October 1987), when three players were sent off.

The trio of Chris Woods, Terry Butcher and Frank McAvennie (along with Graham Roberts, who conducted the Ibrox choir) were all charged and later appeared in court.

Season 1988/89 was special. The foundations of this year would be built upon to become, in time, the house that was *'Nine-in-a-Row'*. But it was also special because of a day in late August when Celtic, the title holders, came

Kevin Drinkell scores Rangers 4th in the 5-1 league defeat of Celtic, August 27, 1988.

Mark Walters scores No. 5 in the same game.

calling. Even with a goal of a start, it was still 'No Contest', as they were swept aside in a blue tidal wave. The final 5-1 scoreline could - and should - have been greater as the 'Gers visibly eased off in the latter stages of the game, when Celtic were in complete disarray and totally demoralised. A similar fate awaited them in the early January encounter but on this occasion, even though Celtic scored first again, the 'Light Blues' could only manage four in reply!

The team in green did win the 'home' ninety minutes (3-1) sandwiched between both famous routs but our conquering heroes returned to the same venue next 'April Fools' Day' to take full points (2-1). A 'treble' now beckoned but, unfortunately, Rangers were denied on Scottish Cup Final day, losing 1-0 to their old rivals. Typically, there was much discussion following the defeat, especially from a Rangers point of view, regarding the merits of some refereeing decisions. This was nothing compared to the sound of voices, from both sides of the fence, that would be heard in early July ....

There had been ample press and TV coverage of the fact that Maurice Johnston was returning to Celtic after his time in France with Nantes. It was something of a coup for the club. Imagine the consternation, therefore, when he was introduced to the awaiting media by Graeme Souness on 10th July, as *Rangers'* latest signing! It was now a case of 'Hold the Front Page' all over the country as the news broke. Certainly, many season ticket holders at the club were not happy, but to others, it was a case of, let's wait and see!

Indeed, the wait was not long. The 'Old Firm' met at Ibrox in early November 1989 on league duty for the second time that season, with spoils shared in the first meeting at 1-1. Near the end, Maurice Johnston scored the game's only goal, his first against his former employers, enabling Rangers to take top spot in the Premier Division for the first time that year. It would seem that the player had arrived.

Full points were taken from the remaining encounters on the way to retaining the league crown (for the first time since 1976) but it was Celtic who progressed in the Scottish Cup (1-0). A strangely similar pattern of events unfolded in season 1990/91, with Rangers dominant in the Championship and their rivals advancing in the major cup competition again, albeit after a horror show in which three men in blue were ordered off in the quarter final. Far less controversially, the League

Cup was regained by beating Celtic 2-1 (goals from Mark Walters and Richard Gough), after initially going behind. With flag No. 41 (a world record), it was double celebration time.

The following year, the bulk of the drama surrounding the sides was confined to a monsoon-engulfed national stadium in late March. Few could have anticipated such a tense evening prior to this Scottish Cup Semi Final Hampden date. Celtic had convincingly won the Premier League encounter 2-0 at Ibrox ten days previously and were, understandably, confident of victory. No doubt that confidence increased when Rangers fullback, David Robertson, was sensationally ordered off after only six minutes! Despite being reduced to ten men, the 'Light Blues' virtually dominated the first half and Ally McCoist scored just before the interval. The second period seemed like an eternity as Celtic, with the extra man and driving wind and rain at their backs, pushed forward. Ten heroes literally ran themselves into the ground that night to produce an epic team performance that has become part of Rangers legend.

Season 1992/93, in 'Old Firm' terms, was mainly notable for the November clash, coming just three days after that historic victory at Elland Road in the European Cup. Despite losing both central defenders, John Brown and Richard Gough, during the game itself, Ian Durrant's first-half goal was enough to take the Parkhead points - thirteen of which separated the teams when the curtain fell.

One year on, as the Ibrox club sought to negotiate the hurdle that was 'Six-in-a-Row', Celtic had come from behind to win 2-1 in Lou Macari's first game in charge. Two months later, on New Year's Day 1994 in the East End of Glasgow, there was little danger of that happening. With less than five minutes on the clock, Rangers had struck twice like a tempest in blue. Celtic were eventually blown away 4-2, with Ukrainians, Mikhailitchenko and Kuznetsov, claiming three goals between them. The first scorer that day was Mark Hateley, who also clinched the winner for ten-man Rangers when the teams met at Ibrox in the League Cup semi final. Two points: 'ten-man' because Pieter Huistra had been sent off for 'doing a Beckham' (ie, a petulant kick) and 'Ibrox' because the national (ie. neutral) stadium was being rebuilt.

The following season, Champions, Rangers, sailed further away from the

Mark Hateley celebrates his first-minute goal against Celtic, New Years Day, 1994.

rowing boat that was Celtic, who finished below both Motherwell and Hibernian in the table. When the sides collided in October, the 'Light Blues' had just lost to Motherwell in the league and the 'Hoops' had disposed of Aberdeen at the 'semi' stage of the 'Coca-Cola' Cup. In theory, Celtic held the advantage but when did theory ever win matches? The reality now was that, when it *really* mattered, Rangers tended to win. The 3-1 scoreline only underlined the fact.

When the clubs met for their first duel in 1995, Celtic led the table by one point and had scored eight goals without loss in the previous two games. Their confidence was high .... and misplaced! Paul Gascoigne's tremendous solo effort (when he ran from his own penalty area to score) was Rangers' second, following a rare headed goal by fullback Alex Cleland in the first half. From a neutral point of view, the 3-3 draw at Ibrox in November had everything, including a miraculous stop by Andy Goram from a point-blank van Hooijdonk volley, with the defence posted missing. In the four league outings that season, Rangers had won two and drawn the others.

The scalp of Celtic had been taken in both 'Cup' encounters that year. Ally

McCoist scored the only goal in the 1-0 'Coca-Cola' Cup victory at Parkhead (November 1995) and 'Follow-Followed' up with the opener when the teams were paired together in the 'semi' of the Scottish Cup. Apart from the win, the undisputed highlight that day was Brian Laudrup's clincher, when he lobbed the Celtic 'keeper from outside the penalty area to complete a majestic, flowing movement. In the eyes of many, it was the goal of the long league and cup campaign.

The pressure would, inevitably, mount as season 1996/97 progressed towards the Holy Grail of *'Nine-in-a-Row'*, which was now so tantalisingly close, just over the horizon. In the 'Old Firm' encounters, Celtic's challenge was brushed aside on all four occasions. Prior to the first game in September, the visitors to Ibrox were still unbeaten in thirty-seven league encounters. Goals from Gough and Gascoigne ensured that the run came to an end. Two months on, Brian Laudrup played to devastating effect on his own 'up front' at Parkhead. The 'Lone Ranger' scored the night's only goal and Andy Goram, magnificent as always, saved a penalty late on.

Even more dramatic was the 'New Year' fixture. With a 1-1 draw seeming the most likely outcome, substitute Erik Bo Andersen struck twice in the last seven minutes for a quite sublime end to the evening. On the afternoon of Sunday 16th March 1997, Celtic had one final chance of stopping Rangers' ultimate goal of equalling their own jealously guarded record of the 1960s and 1970s. Most neutrals were tipping a Celtic victory in the wake of their Scottish Cup triumph over Rangers (2-0) some ten days earlier and the Ibrox club's subsequent 'home' defeat by Dundee United.

Before kick-off, the defending champions were five points ahead of their opponents, with seven games remaining. The Ibrox club's seemingly never-ending injury list (especially in attack) had forced manager Walter Smith into the transfer market with the result that the fans' favourite, Mark Hateley, was back to make his 'debut'.

The only goal of the game, late on in the first half, followed Ian Durrant's cross into the penalty area, which was bundled home by Brian Laudrup. Not the prettiest of goals but .... both Hateley and Celtic defender, Mackay, were red-carded in the second period as the game rapidly deteriorated as a footballing spectacle. It had become a particularly bad-tempered affair, with Celtic's volatile Italian, Paolo di

Canio, in particular, intent on self-destruction.

Perhaps this had, indeed, been the biggest game in Rangers' recent history. Certainly, it virtually ended Celtic's league challenge for the season. *'Nine-in-a-Row'* finally came to pass in Dundee, the *'City of Discovery'*, in early May and Celtic's long-held record of consecutive titles had been equalled.

Season 1997/98 proved to be a huge anti-climax in Championship terms but Rangers were still the dominant force in 'Old Firm' confrontations - in five meetings, they lost only once. Late on, the teams faced each other at Parkhead in the Scottish Cup semi final. Despite the 'home' side's dominance in the first period, there was still no scoring at the interval. Second-half goals from Ally McCoist and Jorg Albertz (an outstanding solo effort) saw Rangers through to another 'Final' day.

In the title race, it was the 'Ne'erday' and 'spring' fixtures that would have the greatest bearing. The 'Light Blues' headed east in early January, four points clear at the top, knowing that a draw would be no great setback. In the event, they played poorly and were beaten 2-0. In winning this traditional fixture for the first time in ten years, Celtic had given themselves a healthy dose of self-belief.

Fast forward to 12th April at Ibrox. By this time, the team in green were three points ahead of the 'Gers and unbeaten since the turn of the year. Stunning goals from both Jonas Thern and Jorg Albertz, without reply, ensured that Ibrox was a wonderful place to be that Sunday.

Sadly, the 'Light Blues' would falter in two of their four remaining league games and thus allow Celtic an easier path to the title. This seemed to sum up Rangers' season but, after nine glorious Championships, it was still hard to take.

And so a decade of dominance and halcyon days ended with their greatest rivals taking the applause. The show goes on, however, with different performers taking the stage. A new era beckons, with a particularly strong Dutch influence.

Brighter, hopefully, than a field of bulbs. . . .

SCOTTISH LEAGUE CHAMPIONSHIP

1891
The Scottish League had been formed for the start of this season with the following founder members:
Rangers, Celtic, Third Lanark, Hearts, St. Mirren, Dumbarton, Renton, Cowlairs, Cambuslang, Vale of Leven and Abercorn. For the record, Rangers' first-ever League match was a 5-2 defeat of Hearts.
After the final fixtures, Rangers and Dumbarton were tied on 29 points each. The resultant play-off ended in a 2-2 draw and, thus, the inaugural Scottish League Championship was shared.

1899
A record-breaking season as the Ibrox club won all eighteen of their league games to lift the title.

1900, 1901 and 1902
Rangers retained the Championship for the following three years and it was *'Four-in-a-Row'*, Victorian-style!

1911
Due to ground work at Ibrox, both games against Celtic were played at Parkhead, with Rangers winning one and drawing the other. In a total of forty-two appearances, centre-forward William Reid netted forty-eight goals for the club.

1912 and 1913
The Championship was retained.

1918
By this time, the *'War to end all Wars'* had taken its toll. It was, therefore, a somewhat less than full-strength collection of teams from which Rangers emerged victorious.

1920
The Championship was decided over forty-two games. The 'Light Blues' suffered only two defeats and scored 106 goals.

1921
The beginning of the 'Struth' era and a campaign in which only one defeat was recorded. Celtic lagged ten point behind in second place.

1923
A twelfth title in Rangers' 50th Anniversary year.

1924 and 1925
The Championship was retained for a further two years.

1927
The Championship was regained after a poor 6th position the previous season.

1928

A 5-1 victory over Kilmarnock finally secured the title, a week after Rangers had lifted the Scottish Cup, beating Celtic 4-0. A great 'double' year.

1929

The Championship was retained.

1930

Never since equalled anywhere in the world, the club won every competition for which they were eligible to enter:
The League Championship, Scottish Cup, Glasgow Cup, Glasgow Charity Cup, Second Eleven Cup and Scottish Alliance (Reserve League Championship).

1931

The Championship was retained for *'Five-in-a-Row'* celebrations.

1933

The season in which the legendary Alan Morton played his last games for Rangers was another Championship triumph. The 'Wee Blue Devil' had been a magnificent club servant, with 495 games and 115 goals to his credit.

1934

Another 'double' year in which Rangers reigned supreme. Also crowned unofficial British Champions following a 2-0 victory over the great Arsenal side of the early thirties.

1935

Yet again, a 'double' year. Winger, Sandy Archibald, ended his career with the club, returning to Raith Rovers. The famous Celtic manager, Willie Maley, had once said that he was never confident of a Celtic victory if Archibald was in the Rangers line-up!

1937

The Championship was regained and it was now number twenty three.

1939

Waddell, Woodburn and Thornton were making their mark as Rangers championed again. The world was changing, however, and by September of that year, Britain and Germany were at war. Europe would never be the same again.

1947

Hibernian were edged out by two points as the 'Light Blues' lifted the first post-war title. This was also the year that the League Cup competition was introduced - Rangers crushed Aberdeen 4-0 in the final.

1949

Not just the Championship but Scotland's first-ever 'treble' of League, League Cup and Scottish Cup. The electric Willie Thornton scored thirty-six goals this season.

1950

A crowd of over 100,000 people at Ibrox watched the penultimate game of the season when Rangers and Hibs drew 0-0. One point 'away' to Third Lanark was all that was now required. The team duly obliged and the League flag flew over Ibrox once again.

1953

A nailbiting finish to the campaign. The club required one point from their final game, 'away' to Queen of the South. Defending champions, Hibernian, would then lose out on goal difference.

Rangers were 1-0 down, with fifteen minutes to play, before Willie Waddell netted the equaliser in dramatic fashion. Having secured the 'golden point', the celebrations began.

1956

Initially the outlook was bleak, as only one of the first six campaign fixtures had been won. Seasons change in more ways than one, however. The controversial Don Kitchenbrand arrived from South Africa and ended the campaign as top league goalscorer with 24 strikes. Nicknamed 'The Rhino', he scored five the night Rangers swamped Queen of the South 8-0. Interestingly, this game was the very first Scottish fixture to be played under floodlights.

1957

The 'Light Blues' had trailed Hearts for most of the season but a sixteen-game unbeaten run at the end won them the title.

1959

A bizarre climax this time round, as Rangers were beaten in their last game of the campaign, at 'home' to Aberdeen. Closest rivals, Hearts, would have taken the title if they had won the same day. In fact, they lost 2-1 - against Celtic at Parkhead. There was many a wry smile in Govan over the next few weeks.

1961

This season witnessed the arrival of Jim Baxter, one of the truly gifted players to wear the blue. Celtic were crushed 5-1 on their home ground, thus establishing a record league victory at Parkhead.

In another outstanding Rangers performance, Hearts were beaten 3-1 at Tynecastle - fullback Bobby Shearer played in goal for 83 minutes after the loss of 'keeper, Billy Ritchie.

The Championship was secured by a one-point margin (from Kilmarnock) following a 7-3 victory over Ayr United on the last day.

1963

The icing on this year's title cake (won by nine points) was the famous Scottish Cup triumph over Celtic. Jim Baxter was a class apart and the 3-0 scoreline hardly reflected Rangers' superiority.

1964

This 34th Championship was part of another magical 'treble' in the season when Rangers won five out five against Celtic. Jim Forrest netted thirty-nine goals, including a record four in the League Cup Final.

Little did the overjoyed fans realise that it would be eleven extremely long years before the League Championship returned to Ibrox.

1975

Celtic's domination of the domestic title scene finally ended at Easter Road on 29th March, when Colin Stein's headed goal against Hibernian claimed a share of the points. This was the last Championship before reconstruction and the formation of the Premier Division.

1976

Rangers were unbeaten in the league from early December until the end of the season. Derek Johnstone's title-clinching goal was scored in a mere 22 seconds at Tannadice against Dundee United. One week later in the Scottish Cup Final, it took him 45 seconds to open the scoring! Another 'treble' year.

1978

Jock Wallace became the first Rangers manager to guide the club to two 'trebles'. Second-placed Aberdeen had, in fact, beaten the Ibrox club in three of their four league fixtures.

1987

Graeme Souness arrived and Scottish football would never be the same again. Rangers were transformed. In his first season, the club came from way behind to clinch the title - in November, Celtic had led by nine points!
Captain Terry Butcher scored the all-important goal at Aberdeen in early May to end the nine-year famine.

1989

'Doubles' from both Kevin Drinkell and Mel Sterland in the 4-0 'home' victory over Hearts secured Rangers' 39th League Flag. The season was also memorable for comprehensive 5-1 and 4-1 victories over Celtic.
Few realised at the time that this was the beginning of a record-equalling 'Nine-in-a-Row' series of League Championship triumphs.

1990

Ex-Celt, Maurice Johnston, arrived to wear the blue and by season's end had notched fifteen league goals, including strikes in the 'home' games against Aberdeen, Hearts and, most famously, Celtic. Rangers won 1-0 on each occasion. Trevor Steven scored the title-winning goal at Tannadice.

1991

Mark Hateley became an Ibrox legend when his double against Aberdeen on the last day of the season snatched the title from the 'Granite City' contenders. A draw would have been sufficient to take the title north.
Walter Smith had replaced Graeme Souness as manager earlier in April.

1992

Ally McCoist, with 34 league goals, became the first Scot to win Europe's prestigious 'Golden Boot' award. It was the year of Rangers' first League and Scottish Cup 'double' since 1978, with the team winning an astonishing 19 out of 22 'away' fixtures in the Championship.

1993
One of the truly great seasons. As well as a domestic 'treble', the 'Light Blues' came so, so close to European glory with an unbeaten run in the 'Champions' League'.

1994
Mark Hateley became the first Englishman to win the Football Writers' 'Player of the Year' award. In an amazing Ne'erday encounter at Parkhead, Rangers were 3-0 ahead after only half an hour - like a hurricane!

1995
Second-placed Motherwell finished 15 points behind as Brian Laudrup baffled opponents and astonished fans throughout Scotland. A 'Player of the Year' in every sense.

1996
An impressive Celtic side only lost one game all season - but it was not enough to stop Rangers. The combination of Gascoigne and Laudrup was too irresistible. Paul's 'hat-trick' against Aberdeen at Ibrox to secure the title will be remembered for many a long year - one of his finest hours in the blue of Rangers.

1997
It was fitting that Brian Laudrup's goal (in the 1-0 Tannadice victory) should land the ultimate prize. Without a doubt, the season had been his. At Tynecastle and Pittodrie in December, the Dane had orchestrated stunning 3-0 and 4-1 victories respectively as well as scoring on each occasion.
At last, Celtic's record had been equalled - *'Nine-in-a-Row'* was finally reality.

THE LEAGUE CAMPAIGNS

Season	P	W	D	L	F	A	Pts	Pos
1890-91	18	13	3	2	58	25	29	1st equal
1891-92	22	11	2	9	59	46	24	5th
1892-93	18	12	4	2	41	27	28	2nd
1893-94	18	8	4	6	44	30	20	4th
1894-95	18	10	2	6	41	26	22	3rd
1895-96	18	11	4	3	57	39	26	2nd
1896-97	18	11	3	4	64	30	25	3rd
1897-98	18	13	3	2	71	15	29	2nd
1898-99	18	18	-	-	79	18	36	1st
1899-1900	18	15	2	1	69	27	32	1st
1900-01	20	17	1	2	60	25	35	1st
1901-02	18	13	2	3	43	29	28	1st
1902-03	22	12	5	5	56	30	29	3rd
1903-04	26	16	6	4	80	33	38	3rd
1904-05	26	19	3	4	83	28	41	2nd
1905-06	30	15	7	8	58	48	37	4th
1906-07	34	19	7	8	69	33	45	3rd
1907-08	34	21	8	5	74	40	50	3rd
1908-09	34	19	7	8	91	38	45	4th
1909-10	34	20	6	8	70	35	46	3rd
1910-11	34	23	6	5	90	34	52	1st
1911-12	34	24	3	7	86	34	51	1st
1912-13	34	24	5	5	76	41	53	1st
1913-14	38	27	5	6	79	31	59	2nd
1914-15	38	23	4	11	74	47	50	3rd
1915-16	38	25	6	7	87	39	56	2nd
1916-17	38	24	5	9	68	32	53	3rd
1917-18	34	25	6	3	66	24	56	1st
1918-19	34	26	5	3	86	16	57	2nd
1919-20	42	31	9	2	106	25	71	1st
1920-21	42	35	6	1	91	24	76	1st
1921-22	42	28	10	4	83	26	66	2nd
1922-23	38	23	9	6	67	29	55	1st
1923-24	38	25	9	4	72	22	59	1st
1924-25	38	25	10	3	76	26	60	1st
1925-26	38	19	6	13	79	55	44	6th
1926-27	38	23	10	5	85	41	56	1st
1927-28	38	26	8	4	109	36	60	1st
1928-29	38	30	7	1	107	32	67	1st
1929-30	38	28	4	6	94	32	60	1st
1930-31	38	27	6	5	96	29	60	1st
1931-32	38	28	5	5	118	42	61	2nd
1932-33	38	26	10	2	113	43	62	1st
1933-34	38	30	6	2	118	41	66	1st
1934-35	38	25	5	8	96	46	55	1st
1935-36	38	27	7	4	110	43	61	2nd
1936-37	38	26	9	3	88	32	61	1st
1937-38	38	18	13	7	75	49	49	3rd

Season	P	W	D	L	F	A	Pts	Pos
1938-39	38	25	9	4	112	55	59	1st
1946-47	30	21	4	5	76	26	46	1st
1947-48	30	21	4	5	64	28	46	2nd
1948-49	30	20	6	4	63	32	46	1st
1949-50	30	22	6	2	58	26	50	1st
1950-51	30	17	4	9	64	37	38	2nd
1951-52	30	16	9	5	61	31	41	2nd
1952-53	30	18	7	5	80	39	43	1st
1953-54	30	13	8	9	56	35	34	4th
1954-55	30	19	3	8	67	33	41	3rd
1955-56	34	22	8	4	85	27	52	1st
1956-57	34	26	3	5	96	48	55	1st
1957-58	34	22	5	7	89	49	49	2nd
1958-59	34	21	8	5	92	51	50	1st
1959-60	34	17	8	9	72	38	42	3rd
1960-61	34	23	5	6	88	46	51	1st
1961-62	34	22	7	5	84	31	51	2nd
1962-63	34	25	7	2	94	28	57	1st
1963-64	34	25	5	4	85	31	55	1st
1964-65	34	18	8	8	78	35	44	5th
1965-66	34	25	5	4	91	29	55	2nd
1966-67	34	24	7	3	92	31	55	2nd
1967-68	34	28	5	1	93	34	61	2nd
1968-69	34	21	7	6	81	32	49	2nd
1969-70	34	19	7	8	67	40	45	2nd
1970-71	34	16	9	9	58	34	41	4th
1971-72	34	21	2	11	71	38	44	3rd
1972-73	34	26	4	4	74	30	56	2nd
1973-74	34	21	6	7	67	34	48	3rd
1974-75	34	25	6	3	86	33	56	1st
1975-76	36	23	8	5	60	24	54	1st
1976-77	36	18	10	8	62	37	46	2nd
1977-78	36	24	7	5	76	39	55	1st
1978-79	36	18	9	9	52	35	45	2nd
1979-80	36	15	7	14	50	46	37	5th
1980-81	36	16	12	8	60	32	44	3rd
1981-82	36	16	11	9	57	45	43	3rd
1982-83	36	13	12	11	52	41	38	4th
1983-84	36	15	12	9	53	41	42	4th
1984-85	36	13	12	11	47	38	38	4th
1985-86	36	13	9	14	53	45	35	5th
1986-87	44	31	7	6	85	23	69	1st
1987-88	44	26	8	10	85	34	60	3rd
1988-89	36	26	4	6	62	26	56	1st
1989-90	36	20	11	5	48	19	51	1st
1990-91	36	24	7	5	62	23	55	1st
1991-92	44	33	6	5	101	31	72	1st
1992-93	44	33	7	4	97	35	73	1st
1993-94	44	22	14	8	74	41	58	1st
1994-95	36	20	9	7	60	35	69	1st
1995-96	36	27	6	3	85	25	87	1st
1996-97	36	25	5	6	85	33	80	1st
1997-98	36	21	9	6	76	38	72	2nd

THE MANAGERS

WILLIAM STRUTH, 1920-1954

League Champions: 1921, 1923, 1924, 1925, 1927, 1928, 1929, 1930, 1931, 1933, 1934, 1935, 1937, 1939, 1947, 1949, 1950, 1953.

Scottish Cup Winners: 1928, 1930, 1932, 1934, 1935, 1936, 1948, 1949, 1950, 1953.

League Cup Winners: 1946-47, 1948-49.

SCOT SYMON, 1954-1967

League Champions: 1956, 1957, 1959, 1961, 1963, 1964.

Scottish Cup Winners: 1960, 1962, 1963, 1964, 1966.

League Cup Winners: 1960-61, 1961-62, 1963-64, 1964-65.

European Cup Winners' Cup: Runners Up 1961, 1967.

DAVID WHITE, 1967-69

Although Jock Stein's Celtic dominated, manager David White came so close to Championship glory in season 1967/68. His team was unbeaten in the league until the last game of the season, when Aberdeen won 3-2 at Ibrox. Celtic won the Championship by two points.

WILLE WADDELL, 1969-72

League Cup Winners: 1970-71.

European Cup Winners' Cup: 1972.

JOCK WALLACE, 1972-1978 & 1983-1986

League Champions: 1975, 1976, 1978.

Scottish Cup Winners: 1973, 1976, 1978.

League Cup Winners: 1975-76, 1977-78, 1983-84, 1984-85.

JOHN GREIG, 1978-83

Scottish Cup Winners: 1979, 1981.

League Cup Winners: 1978-79, 1981-82.

GRAEME SOUNESS, 1986-1991

League Champions: 1987, 1989, 1990.

League Cup Winners: 1986-87, 1987-88, 1988-89, 1990-91.

WALTER SMITH, 1991-1998

League Champions: 1991, 1992, 1993, 1994, 1995, 1996, 1997.

Scottish Cup Winners: 1992, 1993, 1996.

League Cup Winners: 1992-93, 1993-94, 1996-97.

Famous Victories,

an Historic Game

&

Great Players

FAMOUS VICTORIES
SCOTTISH LEAGUE, SEPTEMBER 1960
CELTIC 1, RANGERS 5

WITH the arrival of Jim Baxter from Raith Rovers in late June 1960, manager Scot Symon had signed the player considered by many to be the most gifted footballer ever to wear the blue of Rangers. His influence was immediate and, in many ways, it was the addition of Jim Baxter that transformed the 'Light Bues' from a good side into the great one of the early sixties.

The old foes had already clashed twice in the League Cup qualifying section, with Celtic winning 3-2 at Ibrox and Rangers returning the compliment 2-1 at Parkhead, one week prior to this encounter. Another close match was anticipated by everybody - indeed, few would have foreseen a record scoreline to stand the test of time.

The 'Gers struck early (in only two minutes), with winger Alex Scott giving his side the advantage. That solitary goal separated the teams at the interval. When Jimmy Millar claimed a second with twenty-five minutes left to play, Rangers moved into cruise control and turned on the style, adding another three goals in the space of just seven minutes. Ralph Brand converted a Millar cross before left winger, Davie Wilson, made it four. The magic five was reached when 'Man of the Match', Harold Davis (incidentally, a Korean War veteran), converted an Alex Scott corner with only five minutes remaining. Celtic's consolation goal at the very end was an irrelevance.

This was the start of a memorable season in which Rangers not only lifted the Championship but also became the first British team to reach the final of a European competition. It is worth recalling the line-up in blue that September day:

Ritchie, Shearer, Caldow, Davis, Paterson, Baxter, Scott, McMillan, Millar, Brand and Wilson.

Heroes to a man, their record league win at Parkhead has never been matched.

EUROPEAN CUP WINNERS' CUP FINAL, MAY 1972 RANGERS 3, MOSCOW DYNAMO 2

IN 1961, Rangers became the first British club to reach the final of any European competition, following an impressive run that saw Ferencvaros (Hungary), Borussia Moenchengladbach (West Germany) and Wolves all fall by the wayside on the road to a Cup Winners' Cup date with Fiorentina of Italy. The team from Florence proved too strong, however, winning 2-0 at Ibrox and 2-1 at home for an aggregate victory of 4-1 and the silverware.

It was a similar scenario in 1967, although, this time, the winners, Bayern Munich, just scraped through 1-0 to lift the same trophy in Nuremberg. The 'Light Blues' had reserved their best form for the games leading up to the final, with victories over Glentoran, Borussia Dortmund (the holders), Real Zaragoza (Spain) and the powerful Bulgarians, Slavia Sofia.

Hopefully, season 1971/72 would not follow the same pattern, as Rennes (France), Sporting Lisbon (Portugal), Torino (Italy) and the old foes, the mighty Bayern Munich, were all disposed of on the way to the final. Surely this time Rangers could reproduce the form that had taken them so far?

The Nou Camp stadium in Barcelona was the venue for the 1972 European Cup Winners' Cup Final between Glasgow Rangers and Moscow Dynamo. The Russians had become the first Soviet side to appear in the final of a European competition and were hungry for success.

The Scots dominated from the start and took the lead in twenty-four minutes, when Dave Smith's through ball was swept home by Colin Stein. Just before the break, Willie Johnston headed home from a Smith cross to make it two. Four minutes into the second half, following a massive kick-out by Peter McCloy, Johnston netted his second. Surely the Russians were dead and buried now? Not so, and substitute, Eschtrekov, pulled one back. The Russians poured forward as Rangers defended desperately. Three minutes from time, the Dynamo pressure paid off and they scored again to make it 3-2. It seemed like an eternity before the referee's whistle sounded and it was all over.

After sixteen very long years and eighty-three games, one of the two major European trophies was Ibrox-bound.

Rangers: McCloy, Jardine, Mathieson, Greig, Johnstone, Smith, McLean, Conn, Stein, MacDonald and Johnston.

Postscript: This medal was the only one that 'Man of the Match', Dave Smith, would ever win with Rangers.

Colin Stein scores Rangers' first goal in the 3-2 victory.

Fans celebrate the most famous European victory.

SCOTTISH CUP FINAL, MAY 1973
RANGERS 3, CELTIC 2

DESPITE Rangers' rich vein of form in the Championship race of season 1972/73 (sixteen successive victories before drawing with Aberdeen at Pittodrie in late April), it was still the team in green who took the title (albeit by just one point) for the eighth year in a row. Although the previous year's wonderful campaign and 'final' success in the European Cup Winners' Cup was still fresh in the minds of the 'Follow-Followers', sadly Kai Johansen's dramatic winner against Celtic, when the team last lifted the Scottish Cup in 1966, was but a distant memory. Now, for the third time in only five years, the 'Old Firm' were ready to do battle on Cup Final day. Over 122,000 fans would witness a classic contest.

Celtic's early dominance paid off when Kenny Dalglish scored from a through ball in just twenty four minutes. Some ten minutes later, Willie Mathieson fed Alex MacDonald and the midfielder's subsequent cross was headed home by Derek Parlane to ensure that it was all square at the interval. Amazingly, only twenty seconds of the second half had elapsed before the 'Light Blues' struck again, with Alfie Conn netting after Parlane and 'Cutty' Young had combined. This lead was short-lived, however, as the 'Eastenders' drew level several minutes later through a Connelly penalty after John Greig had handled on the goal-line.

The winner was quite bizarre but nonetheless memorable. One of Tommy McLean's meticulous crosses - were they ever anything else? - was headed onto the post by Derek Johnstone. As if in slow motion, with the players frozen in time, the ball rolled along the goal-line and struck the other post. Tom Forsyth was the quickest to react and he 'soled' it home from all of six inches for his first-ever Rangers goal.

In the remaining thirty minutes, Conn and MacDonald both spurned chances before it ended 3-2 with the 'Gers well in control. The Centenary Scottish Cup would soon be on its way to Ibrox.

Rangers: McCloy, Jardine, Mathieson, Greig, Johnstone, MacDonald, McLean, Forsyth, Parlane, Conn and Young.

Postscript:

Alfie Conn, the scorer of No. 2, committed the 'ultimate sin' in March 1977 when he joined Celtic via Tottenham Hotspur. That same year, the player was part of the team which defeated Rangers 1-0 .... in the Scottish Cup Final.

SCOTTISH CUP FINAL (REPLAY), MAY 1981
RANGERS 4, DUNDEE UNITED 1

IN TRUTH, the Scottish Cup had become something of an embarrassment for the club. After all, Rangers had reached the final of the tournament in successive years since season 1975/76 only to fall at this 'final' hurdle, not only to Celtic (on two separate occasions) but to Hearts, Aberdeen and Hibernian as well.

On the road to Hampden that year, the 'Light Blues' had survived a real scare 'away' to St. Johnstone in the fourth round. With the score at 3-2 in favour of the home side, Ian Redford's last-minute equaliser ensured a replay as opposed to a humiliating defeat. Four days later, Rangers won 3-1.

Final opponents, Dundee United, had already won the League Cup (for the previous two years) and were very much favourites to lift this trophy. Indeed, the 'Tangerines' were the dominant force for much of the first game without managing to score. All would change, however, with some ten minutes left on the clock and the introduction of David Cooper and John MacDonald. This 'new' Rangers created several chances before, in the last minute, Bobby Russell was brought down in the box for an undisputed penalty. Although Ian Redford (the Perth saviour) had already beaten goalkeeper McAlpine from the spot in the league (2-1, Ibrox 4.4.81), on this occasion the United 'keeper saved. Extra time being of no consequence, a replay was scheduled for four days later.

This time it would be oh so different, as manager John Greig brought back Derek Johnstone and played both Davie Cooper and John MacDonald from the start. The difference was night and day.

Within twenty minutes, the 'Light Blues' were two up, with Davie Cooper instrumental in both. He clipped home the first himself and then, following the winger's free kick, Bobby Russell struck the second. Although Dodds pulled one back, it was 3-1 at the interval after John MacDonald converted from a quite magnificent Cooper pass. In that first forty-five, Davie had been truly awe-inspiring, ripping the United defence to shreds.

There was little danger of a Tayside revival when the teams returned to the field and, indeed, John MacDonald scored a fourth with less than fifteen minutes remaining. Strangely enough, Dundee United had won by the same 4-1 scoreline at Ibrox in March but this victory was far more important, considering previous Cup Final results. Many 'Follow-Followers' felt that the name 'Cooper' should be inscribed alongside that of Rangers on the silverware, such was his golden performance.

Few will ever forget that warm evening and the legend that is Davie Cooper.

Rangers: Stewart, Jardine, Dawson, Stevens, Forsyth, Bett, Cooper, Russell, Johnstone, Redford and MacDonald.

SCOTTISH LEAGUE, APRIL 1990
RANGERS 3, CELTIC 0

SOMETIMES it is easier to win a Championship than to retain it. Although Rangers had established a commanding lead at the top of the league table early on, they were now struggling, as draws against Dundee, St. Mirren, Motherwell and Hearts over the previous six weeks had shown. Worse still, Hibernian had won at Ibrox (1-0) immediately before Celtic's visit. The team from Glasgow's East End were naturally buoyant, after halting Rangers' Scottish Cup progress in late February, and now the old adversaries would meet again on this 'Day of Fools'.

Although the visitors began well, it was Rangers who drew first blood. Following Terry Butcher's hoisted cross into the box, Richard Gough jumped with defender Anton Rogan. Inexplicably, Rogan handled. Maybe he was waving to a friend in the crowd, maybe it was an elaborate April Fools' Day joke but a penalty it *certainly* was. Mark Walters' low, right-foot strike opened the scoring.

Goal number two was a beauty - a half volley from Mo Johnston that left Bonner helpless. This was the striker's second against his former club following Graeme Souness' controversial capture of the player the previous summer from under the nose of Celtic. The 'Light Blues' were now looking the part.

Although the second half was a formality, history was still in the making. A second penalty was awarded when Grant fouled Mo Johnston in the area as he attempted to reach a Mark Walters' cross. It was a chance for Ally McCoist to break the Ibrox post-war record of league goals, jointly held with Derek Johnstone. He did.

For Rangers, the 3-0 victory was paramount in ensuring that the title was retained (for the first time since 1976). For Celtic, their days in the Championship wilderness were only just beginning.

Rangers: Woods, Stevens, Munro, Gough, Spackman, Butcher, Steven, Ferguson, McCoist, Johnston and Walters.

SCOTTISH CUP SEMI FINAL, MARCH 1992 RANGERS 1, CELTIC 0

NOT for the first time had the Scottish Cup been an elusive lady to bed. The national trophy had not graced the Ibrox Trophy Room since 1981 when the cup campaign of season 1991/92 got underway. Stern tests would follow at Pittodrie in the third round (1-0, with Ally McCoist scoring his 25th goal of the season), against holders Motherwell at Ibrox (2-1, although the visitors led at half-time) and 'away' to St. Johnstone in the quarter final (3-0, with winger, Pieter Huistra, outstanding). Now it was old 'friends' Celtic at the 'semi' stage.

Certainly, Rangers did not have their problems to seek - Mark Hateley had injured his back in the last minute of the St. Johnstone match at Perth and was out. Both Stuart McCall and Dale Gordon had missed the same game through injury and were struggling to make the side. Oh, yes .... there was also the small matter of Celtic's 2-0 Ibrox triumph ten days before!

The game, played in a howling gale of fierce driving rain, had barely settled when defender David Robertson was sensationally shown the 'red card' for a body check on winger Joe Miller. Only six minutes had been played but, to be fair, it was a rather blatant foul.

Despite the loss of the attacking fullback, Rangers, surprisingly, dominated the first period, which was drawing to a close when Ally McCoist struck. His record 30th goal of the season started with Stuart McCall's precision pass and ended with the striker shooting low past Gordon Marshall from just outside the penalty box.

Celtic's manpower advantage was reinforced in the second 'forty-five' by the monsoon, which was now at their backs but this Rangers outfit was made of sterner stuff, the 'true grit' of Marshal Rooster Cogburn! True, Andy Goram had felt both his post and crossbar judder in separate attacks as the 'Light Blues' defied their opponents and the elements.

Finally, it was all over. Despite the atrocious conditions, the players stayed on the Hampden turf for some ten minutes to acknowledge a devoted support that had, once again, given them incredible vocal backing throughout the tie.

Rangers: Goram, Stevens, Robertson, Gough, Spackman, Brown, Gordon (Rideout, 77mins), McCall, McCoist, Durrant and Huistra.

EUROPEAN CUP, NOVEMBER 1992
LEEDS 1, RANGERS 2

IT WAS just a pointless exercise, a complete and utter waste of time. According to the English press, certainly. Despite the fact that Rangers had won the first leg of the second-round European Cup tie at Ibrox, south of the border, they had already been written off well in advance of their journey to the Midlands.

The 'Light Blues' came from behind in Govan, eventually triumphing 2-1 courtesy of Ally McCoist's winner. Leeds had actually silenced the massed choirs as early as the first minute when Gary McAllister thundered home following a corner. The stage was now set for an intriguing encounter at Elland Road.

Neither set of supporters had been able to purchase tickets for the 'away' game due to concern regarding the possibility of crowd violence. Needless to say, more than a few who followed the blue were there that night to witness quite an extraordinary start to the ninety minutes. The game had barely settled when Mark Hateley's vicious strike arced and dipped behind the Leeds 'keeper, John Lukic, to give Rangers the lead. Quite simply, depending upon your point of view, it was either a fluke or the goal of the season. Certainly some visitors with dulcet Scottish tones came to the latter conclusion and were ejected into the night, still celebrating.

Regardless of any debate, Rangers were now 3-1 ahead (on aggregate) and had forced opposing manager, Howard Wilkinson, into a major tactical re-think. This would be to no avail, however, as the 'Light Blues' began oozing confidence and assuredly took control for the rest of the first half.

Soon after the break, the game ended as an actual contest when the visitors scored again. Ian Durrant and Hateley combined on the left before 'Attila's' beautifully judged, curling cross away from the 'keeper was headed home by Ally McCoist.

Certainly, the immense Andy Goram was finally beaten by Eric Cantona (before his poetic 'trawler' days with Manchester United) right at the end but, by then, it was definitely all over bar the shouting .... or the silence!

This had been one of Rangers' great European nights on English soil in a season when even teams with the pedigree of Marseille , CSKA Moscow and FC Brugge would fail to inflict defeat on the Scottish Champions.

Although the year would be littered with numerous highlights on the road to a coveted domestic 'treble' of League Championship, Scottish Cup and League Cup (for only the first time since 1978), in the eyes of many nothing compared to a certain November night in a rather grey part of the kingdom.

SCOTTISH LEAGUE CUP FINAL, OCTOBER 1993
HIBERNIAN 1, RANGERS 2

Ally McCoist's stunning winning goal.

STRANGELY enough, Rangers and Hibernian had never met at this 'final' stage of the League Cup competition in its entire history. Certainly, the sides had clashed (on semi-final night) as recently as 1991, the year in which the Edinburgh club delivered the trophy to their long-suffering support.

The 'Light Blues' had a record second to none in this competition over the previous decade, having reached the final every season bar two. On both those occasions (1986 and the aforementioned 1991), it was - surprise, surprise - Hibs who extinguished the blue light. Understandably, the east of Scotland outfit entertained thoughts of a unique 'hat-trick' prior to the confrontation. After all, with twelve games played, they led the Championship race (by two points from Rangers) and were playing well.

After forty-five minutes, both teams left the field with neither having gained the advantage. Ten minutes into the second period, the deadlock was broken when Ian

Durrant gave the 'Light Blues' the lead, deftly lifting the ball over 'keeper Jim Leighton's slim, advancing frame. (One of Govan's favourite sons, Ian Durrant always had a special place in the hearts and minds of Rangers fans and memories of Pittordrie, in October 1988, were never far from their minds).

Almost immediately, Hibs hit back. Well, maybe not quite 'hit back' as it was a ludicrous own goal by Dave McPherson that breathed life into the green shirts again. Sensing that this could be their day, the league leaders pushed forward and, indeed, would have taken the lead but for a Gary Stevens goal-line clearance minutes later.

So the scene was set for a hero to emerge when a less than 100% fit Ally McCoist appeared as substitute, replacing Pieter Huistra. With extra time looming, the McCoist magic cast its spell in the most dramatic fashion. David Robertson's long throw reached a crowded penalty area where Ally, despite his green shadows, executed an audacious overhead kick and Hibs were beaten. The player, idolised by the Ibrox legions for many a season, had done it again.

Not for the last time, would the name of Alistair McCoist be linked with that of saviour. Even in his last season with the club, more than anything else, it was his 'never-say-die' attitude that lifted the team when all seemed lost in the latter weeks of the 1997/98 Championship and Scottish Cup campaigns. A rare breed, indeed.

Rangers: Maxwell, Stevens, Robertson, Gough, McPherson, McCall, Steven, Durrant, Hateley, Huistra (McCoist).

SCOTTISH LEAGUE, APRIL 1996
RANGERS 3, ABERDEEN 1

NOTHING had been decided. With two games remaining, Rangers were still only one point ahead of Celtic, although the Parkhead club were just ninety minutes away from completing *their* league programme. To be fair, the 'Eastenders' had been a model of consistency that season, losing only once throughout the entire campaign to date. Something which not even the 'Light Blues' had achieved.

Nonetheless, the facts were simple: defeat Aberdeen at Ibrox on 28th April and Championship Flag No. 46 could be unfurled. Incentive enough. Of course, the team from the 'Granite City' had no intentions of being lambs to the slaughter and, as if to prove the point, duly opened the scoring in nineteen minutes with a goal from centre-half, Brian Irvine. Their smiles faded quickly, however, as Rangers hit back almost immediately in the person of Scotland's 'Player of the Year', Paul Gascoigne.

Paul Gascoigne's first goal against Aberdeen at Ibrox, April 28, 1996.

Collecting Brian Laudrup's corner on the edge of the penalty area, the midfield maestro eased past strikers Dodds and Windass, before curling the ball high past 'keeper, Michael Watt, for the equaliser. Quite superb - but better, much better, was still to come.

Although Rangers were now the driving force, luck was not with them when the woodwork denied Alan McLaren on two separate occasions. With a draw seeming the most likely outcome, the words 'Gascoigne' and 'genius' came together. And £4.3 million seemed a paltry sum, indeed.

With nine minutes to go, the joking 'Geordie' took possession in his own half and set off for the Aberdeen goal. Like Moses parting the Red Sea, resistance was futile, as challenge after challenge was brushed aside before a precise left-foot shot and Watt was helpless. Ibrox erupted.

Even then, it was not quite all over as there was still enough time for 'Gazza' to claim his 'hat-trick' after Gordon Durie had been brought down for an obvious penalty. By this time, of course, 'Eight-in-a-Row' celebrations were already in full swing.

Paul Gascoigne was never far from the spotlight during his three-year period with the club. This was the day when his light shone brightest by far and over 47,000 fans were privileged to witness one of the greatest individual performances ever seen inside the Stadium. And that goal?

Goal of the season, certainly. Goal of the decade, just maybe.

Rangers: Goram, Steven (Petric), Robertson, Gough, McLaren, Brown, Durie (Durrant), Gascoigne, Andersen (McCoist), McCall, Laudrup.

The players celebrate Gazza's 'hat-trick'.

SCOTTISH CUP FINAL, MAY 1996
RANGERS 5, HEARTS 1

RANGERS had met no-one of any substance in the Scottish Cup run of 1996 until old friends, Celtic, appeared on semi-final day in April. The 'Eastenders' had demolished Aberdeen 5-0 a week earlier in the Premier League and were still shadowing Rangers in the Championship race. Even though their confidence was justifiably high, after ninety minutes, it was the 'Light Blues' who marched on to meet Hearts in the final. Strikes from Ally McCoist and Brian Laudrup (an absolute gem and contender for 'Goal of the Season') were enough to see Rangers home and dry.

Gough and Gascoigne celebrate with 'hat-trick' hero Durie.

Most neutrals had forecast a close encounter, with even a brave few suggesting glory for the 'Gorgie Roaders'. Annihilation of the 'Maroons', however, was just not a possibility.

In thirty-seven minutes, the Champions were ahead. Following good lead-up work by Gordon Durie, the 'Great Dane', Brian Laudrup, rifled home past Rousset with clinical efficiency for the only goal of the first period. Just after the break, the Frenchman was again picking the ball out of his own net after having blundered - a rather innocuous Brian Laudrup cross slipping through his legs. Quel damage!

The 'Light Blues' now had the scent of victory in their nostrils and, as Gordon Durie moved into the spotlight, proceeded to take Hearts apart. The striker's first goal of the afternoon, in sixty-six minutes, was a volley on the run following Laudrup's cross. Colquhoun's reply for Hearts was only a diversion at this stage.

After netting from close range, Durie claimed his third, heading home with five minutes to play. The Scottish Cup Final had just witnessed its first 'hat-trick' since 1972 and, indeed, only the third in the competition's entire history. Most accolades, nevertheless, fell in the direction of Walter Smith's finest-ever signing, who not only scored twice but created all the others that day.

In years to come, this game would simply be known as the 'hour of Brian Laudrup'.

Gordon Durie scores his second.

HISTORIC GAME
RANGERS v MOSCOW DYNAMO, NOVEMBER 1945

WITH the upsurge in attendances as the nation and football slowly returned to normality after the end of the Second World War, demand for 'glamour' games increased. Moscow Dynamo, the pride of the Soviet Union, were touring Great Britain and had agreed to play Rangers in their final game.

The Russians had been most impressive in their three previous outings, dominating Chelsea, although the game was drawn, humiliating Cardiff City 10-1 and beating Arsenal, even though the 'Londoners' included guest stars such as the famous Blackpool duo of Stanley Matthews and Stan Mortensen. Officials accompanying the tourists actually complained about the number of 'guests' Arsenal had in their line-up. Some 'friendly'!

Demand was so great that 3/6d (17½p) enclosure tickets were rumoured to be selling for £1 in the streets around Ibrox. In any event, 90,000 spectators were packed inside the Stadium for a Wednesday afternoon kick-off on 28th November.

In just two minutes, the visitors were ahead through No. 8 Kartsev, whose thunderous twenty-yard free kick left 'keeper, Jerry Dawson, well beaten. Five minutes later, Rangers were awarded a penalty but Willie Waddell's spot kick was saved by 'Tiger' Khomich, the Russian No. 1. It came as little surprise when Dynamo scored again, such was the standard of their play, and it was that man Kartsev again, finishing off a flowing movement. The 'Light Blues' hit back immediately to make a real game of it, when centre-forward, Jimmy Smith, netted from a goalmouth scramble.

The second half was all Rangers, with both Waddell and Charlie Johnstone causing chaos down the flanks. When the latter player was brought down for a second penalty, this time George Young stepped forward .... and he made no mistake. Despite further Rangers pressure, the red rearguard held firm and the game ended in a 2-2 draw. It had been a wonderful afternoon of football.

The 'Light Blues' would return the compliment in the summer of 1962 on their historic tour of Russia. After defeating both Lokomotiv Moscow and Dynamo Tbilisi, the Ibrox club's final game with champions, Dynamo Kiev, ended in a 1-1 draw. Such was the quality of these performances that the crowds increased dramatically from 20,000 in the first game to 60,000 in the last.

Postscript: During the second half of the match in Glasgow, Bobrov (Dynamo's No. 10) was substituted, with Dementiev coming on in his place. Someone had obviously forgotten to tell the player and, for a few minutes, Dynamo had twelve men against eleven.

It was only when the mistake was pointed out to the referee by some Rangers players that Bobrov left the field.

My father, who was at the game, told me this was a deliberate ploy on the Russians' part and, if unchecked, they would have continued with the extra man 'ad infinitum'!

Rangers: Dawson, Gray, Shaw, Watkins, Young, Symon, Waddell, Gillick, Smith (Duncanson), Williamson, Johnstone.

Dynamo goalkeeper Khomich punches clear during a Rangers attack.

Russian cameramen filming at Ibrox.

GREAT PLAYERS

WILLIE WADDELL

WILLIE WADDELL was an outstanding success with the club, both as player and manager. On the field, he scored 143 goals (in 558 first-team appearances) and, of course, as boss, Waddell led Rangers to European glory in 1972.

It began with a first-team appearance at the ripe old age of seventeen against Arsenal in 1938. In this pre-season 'friendly', the 'Gunners' (and England) left-back, Ernie Hapgood, was given a torrid time. Not for the last time, would a defender welcome the sound of the final whistle! In addition to his many goals, the player's crosses from the right wing were converted on numerous occasions by centre-forward, Willie Thornton - the pair were a quite lethal duo.

At international level, a total of 27 'Caps' were awarded before the winger retired from playing in 1956. As manager of Kilmarnock, Waddell took the Ayrshire team to the Championship in 1965 before returning to Rangers in the same capacity, following the sacking of Davie White in November 1969.

Although only managing the 'Light Blues' for some two-and-a-half years, it was Waddell's team that lifted the European Cup Winners' Cup in 1972 for their greatest-ever triumph. He became general manager prior to season 1972/73, with coach, Jock Wallace being promoted at the same time.

Even now, older supporters can still recall the sense of anticipation that filled the Ibrox air when Waddell was in full flight.

JIM BAXTER

IN the eyes of many, Jim Baxter was touched by genius, the most naturally gifted Ranger of them all. Manager Scot Symon brought the player to Ibrox from Raith Rovers in the summer of 1960 for a Scottish record fee of £17,500. The orchestra had found its conductor.

Almost immediately, 'Slim Jim' became an integral part of the Rangers team that would dominate Scottish football in the early sixties and, nearly forty years on, is still considered to be one of the greatest sides in the club's long and illustrious history.

Worshipped both for his supreme left-foot skills and 'Mickey-taking' abilities, midfielder Baxter excelled in the heat of 'Old Firm' infernos. Early on, in that first season of 1960/61, the 'Light Blues' crushed Celtic 5-1 at Parkhead to record their most impressive league victory at that venue. Championship medal No. 1 was confirmed by late April, to be followed by two others in 1963 and 1964.

In the Scottish Cup Final replay of 1963, Celtic were merely the audience to a Baxter performance, although no applause was forthcoming. He ran the show from start to finish and, such was the dominance of the men in blue, that, even with some twenty minutes still to play, the Celtic fans deserted the Hampden slopes en masse, having suffered enough. Rangers won 3-0.

One of the player's best-remembered games in the dark blue (he won 34 'Caps') was against England at Wembley in 1963, when he tormented the life out of those conceited white shirts and also scored both goals in a 2-1 carnival.

After early success in season 1964/65 (Baxter captained the 'Light Blues' to a 2-1

League Cup Final victory over Celtic), tragedy struck further afield in Europe when, late on in the 'away' game with Rapid Vienna, he suffered a leg break. It was the beginning of the end and, in May 1965, the player was sold to Sunderland for £72,000 much to the utter dismay of the 'Follow-Followers'. He returned to the club in May 1969 on a free transfer but was released by new manager, Willie Waddell, at the end of that season, after just one year.

His days with Rangers were finally over but the legend lives on. One thing is certain–we will never see his like again.

JOHN GREIG

JOHN GREIG is a Rangers legend, of that there is no doubt. More than any other post-war player, he embodied the true spirit of the club. A natural leader, with a quite staggering 857 appearances in the blue to his credit, John's first game was against Airdrie in the League Cup of September 1961. He scored on his debut.

Greig won the first of his five Championship medals in 1963, by which time he was an integral part of the Rangers defence. When Celtic reigned supreme in Scotland and were winning their own version of *'Nine-in-a-Row'*, in many ways it was John who, as a truly inspiring Club Captain, held the team together. Even though injured, he was rightly present at Easter Road in April 1975, when the Championship was regained after that long, barren period in Celtic's shadow. Appearing on the park for the last few minutes, he was given a hero's welcome.

Probably the abiding image of John Greig is with the European Cup Winners' Cup on a lap of honour at Ibrox after that glorious night in Barcelona. The beard disappeared soon after! The player of course, also wore the dark blue of Scotland to great effect on many occasions - forty-four, to be exact.

Following the shock resignation of Jock Wallace in late May 1978, it was a case of Club Captain one day, manager the next. Both the Scottish and League Cups were won twice during his five years in the hot seat but the Championship was never realised and, on 28th October 1983, John Greig resigned.

As a player and captain of Rangers, however, he stands tall with the very best of them. There can be no higher praise.

DEREK JOHNSTONE

Young Derek Johnstone scores the winner against Celtic in the League Cup Final of 1970.

FEW players excel in the blue of Rangers in more than one position. Derek Johnstone is one of that rare breed - having worn the colours to great effect at centre-forward, centre-half and in midfield!

After signing as a schoolboy in 1968, the big lad turned professional in 1970. In September of that year, he scored twice on his senior debut against Cowdenbeath at Ibrox. One month later, Derek Johnstone's name was on everyone's lips.

His goal in the League Cup Final victory over Celtic is now the stuff of legend. Not quite seventeen years old, Johnstone became the youngest player to score the winning goal in a cup final. More importantly, Rangers had just won their first major trophy in more than four years.

An impressive medal collection comprises three League Championships (1975, 1976 and 1978), five Scottish Cups (1973, 1976, 1978, 1979 and 1981) and five League Cups, in seasons 1970/71, 1975/76, 1977/78, 1978/79 and 1981/82. Of course, there is also his European Cup Winners' Cup medal of 1972.

It should be remembered that 'DJ' not only scored as a centre-forward and centre-half in separate Scottish Cup Finals but also that the Ranger won Scottish Cup medals in three different positions - the two aforementioned and in midfield!

Although Johnstone was part of Rangers' 'treble'-winning teams of 1976 and 1978, a game outwith this period is often recalled. The player (along with Davie Cooper and John MacDonald) was dropped for the 1981 Scottish Cup Final against Dundee United.

The game ended 0-0. All three returned for the replay, which saw a superb Rangers performance leave the Taysiders reeling. The trophy was won on a 4-1 scoreline.

Chelsea paid £30,000 for his services in 1983 but, in January 1985, Jock Wallace brought him back to Ibrox. The arrival of Graeme Souness finally ended his Rangers career.

Derek Johnstone will always be remembered for his versatility - not only as a deadly finisher but also as a magnificent stopper in the centre of defence.

DAVIE COOPER

ONE of Rangers' most favoured and gifted sons, the supremely talented winger signed from Clydebank in June 1977 for £100,000 after starring for the 'Bankies' in three League Cup ties against the 'Light Blues' the previous season. Within one year, Rangers had lifted the domestic 'treble', with 'Coop' claiming his first 'Old Firm' stripe after scoring in the 2-1 League Cup Final triumph.

Memorable enough as this strike surely was, it was nothing really when you consider his next 'Final' goal against Celtic. In the Drybrough Cup Final of 1979, Davie scored his famous 'Brazilian' goal, juggling past four defenders in green before netting.

Probably the game that fans remember the most - and rightly so - is the 1981 Scottish Cup Final replay against Dundee United, when, on a warm, balmy evening in May, he tore the heart and soul from a Tayside rearguard incapable of stopping him. As well as being a superb crosser of the ball, Davie could unleash quite venomous shots at goal, as witnessed by his ferocious free kick in the League Cup Final of 1987 against Aberdeen.

Something of an enigma, however, sometimes he was mesmerising in one game and totally frustrating the next. It was often said that if Davie Cooper was on form, so were Rangers.

The player joined Motherwell in 1989, enjoying a new lease of life and producing many vintage performances for the Lanarkshire team. Then, in 1993, he returned to his first club, Clydebank, and the circle was complete.

The tragic news that Davie Cooper had passed away on 23rd March 1995 (following a brain haemorrhage the day before) tore a hole in the hearts of thousands. And not just followers of the blue. First and foremost a Rangers man, Davie Cooper was, and always will be, a major part of the club and its history. In a very special sense, he had never really left Ibrox.

TERRY BUTCHER

THE towering 6'4" deputy captain of England arrived at Ibrox from Ipswich town in August 1986 with a formidable reputation. Under the management of Graeme Souness, the central defender would soon become the heart of the new-look Rangers team being assembled at Ibrox. In many ways, he would be Souness' most important signing.

Under Butcher's captaincy, the League Cup was regained in year one, with Celtic 2-1 beaten finalists. It was fitting that, on Championship day at Pittodrie in early May, it was one of his rare goals that secured the required point in a 1-1 draw. It was also Rangers' first title win in nine years. Only twenty-three league goals had been conceded that season, compared to an incredible forty-five the year before!

In the October of season 1987/88, the player was red-carded during the infamous 'Old Firm' clash at Ibrox. Worse would follow one month later, when Butcher broke his left leg against Aberdeen. The season was over and Celtic would go on to lift the title.

Back in action for the next year's campaign, life for both player and club returned to winning normality, with both the Championship and League Cup returning to Govan. Season 1989/90 and Tannadice was the venue (in April) when title No. 40 was confirmed, in a year when only a miserly nineteen goals were given away in thirty-six games.

At this stage, it was hard to imagine the Rangers defence without Butcher at its core but it became a fact prior to the League Cup Final of October 1990. After falling out with the manager, the player was literally sent to Coventry and signed for the Midlands club. It was a sad end to his distinguished career north of the border. To this day, Terry Butcher holds a special place in the hearts of all 'Follow-Followers'.

An Englishman who became a 'True Blue'.

MARK HATELEY

IT IS common knowledge that Mark Hateley did not exactly receive the warmest of welcomes when he first wore the blue of Rangers at the start of season 1990/91. In fact, a minority of so-called supporters were downright hostile to the striker, who had spent most of the previous year (at Monaco) trying to shake off a troublesome ankle injury and was, obviously, far from being 100% fit. Just imagine, though, questioning the ability of someone who had spent three years with AC Milan and played regularly at the very highest level!

Those initial shouts of abuse would return to haunt them, however, when, in early May, the 'Big Man's' two goals against Aberdeen at Ibrox delivered the Championship. His first strike that day (a fifteen-yard header) is now the very stuff of legend.

Hateley's next campaign began with a 'hat-trick' against St. Johnstone (6-0, 10.8.91) and then, more famously, on a rare hot late-August afternoon, the striker claimed both Rangers goals at Parkhead in the 2-0 victory. This period also ended on a high with the player scoring Rangers' first in the Scottish Cup Final against Airdrie (2-1, 9.5.92), when the trophy returned to Ibrox for the first time since 1981.

In season 1992/93, Mark Hateley provided a seemingly endless list of highlights ..... the magnificent left-foot volley from 25 yards at Elland Road against Leeds in the European Cup, the ball nesting in the back of the net even before 'keeper Lukic had returned to earth .... the inch-perfect curling cross for Ally's diving header and goal No. 2 in the same game ...... Mark's own headed equaliser against Marseille that almost took the roof off Ibrox .... another perfect header against Aberdeen at Pittodrie in February to secure the points and severely dent the Dons' title challenge ..... the burst of pace, superb run and sweet, low, shot from an acute angle, for Rangers' second and decisive Cup Final goal. Who was it questioned his ability?

'Attila' was now the most feared striker in Scottish football. He was voted 'Player of the Year' by the Scottish Football Writers' Association at the end of season 1993/94, thus becoming the first Englishman to win this prestigious award. Hateley had totalled thirty goals in all competitions that year, with both Celtic and Aberdeen suffering again. Most fans still recall the opener, in just one minute, at Parkhead on 1st January, when the home side were blown away by four goals to two.

Unfortunately, injury played a major part in his last year with the club and, at the beginning of season 1995/96, Hateley joined Queen's Park Rangers, then bossed by former colleague, Ray Wilkins. That was not quite the end of the story, however, as the player did return briefly to help the cause prior to the 'Nine-in-a-Row' decider at Celtic Park.

Even though Mark only lasted some 66 minutes, he undoubtedly played his part in a momentous Rangers victory. To say that the Celtic defence had no answers to the questions he posed them is an understatement. It was an absolute joy to see him leading the line as only he can.

No greater compliment can be paid.

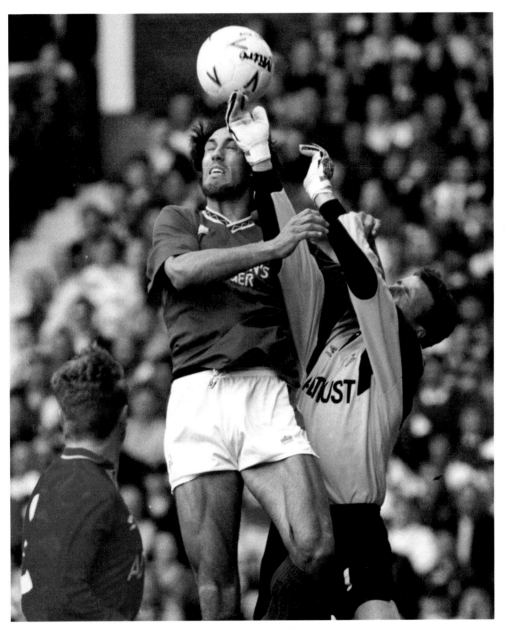

Mark Hateley in the thick of things as usual.

PAUL GASCOIGNE

THERE were many raised eyebrows in the summer of 1995 when Rangers announced that they had completed the signing of wayward genius, Paul Gascoigne, from 'Serie A' club, Lazio, for £4.3 million. His pedigree was never in doubt, just the fact that the 'Geordie' had only played 47 games in three seasons in Italy, having spent a fair percentage of time on the injury list.

In his first season in Glasgow, Paul netted 19 times in 41 games, including quite sublime goals against Celtic at both Ibrox and Parkhead. Probably three of his most celebrated strikes came in the Championship decider against Aberdeen in late April - his performance that day is still spoken of with awe. It came as little surprise when the Ranger was named 'Player of the Year' by both the Scottish Football Writers' Association and his fellow professionals. Obviously it was not just the legions in blue who admired his close control and ability to take on defenders.

Although, the following year, the name 'Gascoigne' seemed to appear more on the front pages than the back, there was still much to admire on the park in a footballing sense. Indeed, it was two flashes of his genius that decided the ultimate destination of November's 'Coca-Cola' Cup, when Rangers met Hearts in the final. Against the same team, one month later, the Englishman ran the show in the 'Light Blues' emphatic 4-1 Tynecastle victory. Although it was the year of Brian Laudrup, Paul, too, had played his part and was there at Tannadice on 7th May for the ultimate triumph.

The player never completed another full season with the club, making only fourteen league appearances (it would certainly have been more but for a lengthy suspension following his 'red card' against Celtic in November) and scoring just three goals in 1997-98 before being transferred to Middlesbrough for approximately £3.5 million in March 1998.

At the end of the day, Paul Gascoigne's contribution to two Championships in three seasons will not be forgotten by the masses that idolised him during his all-too-brief time in Scotland.

ALLY McCOIST

SURPRISING as it may seem, goalscorer supreme, Alistair McCoist, was not always idolised down Govan way. After signing for Rangers in June 1983 (having previously rejected their advances on two separate occasions), many fans, understandably, questioned the player's commitment to the club. The striker worked hard to win over their support and the rest, as they say, is history.

Ally was top scorer for six consecutive seasons from 1983/84 to 1988/89, netting 35, 25, 41, 41, 49 and 25 goals respectively. Impressive enough but period 1991/92 was truly amazing. Apart from heading the 'striking' charts with 41, he also claimed his 200th Scottish League goal and Rangers' 100th of the Championship in the last game of the campaign, 'away' to Aberdeen. The prestigious European 'Golden Boot' trophy joined both Scottish 'Player of the Year' awards in the McCoist household. One year on, he became the only player ever to retain the 'Golden Boot' with 34 goals in 34 games.

A bad leg break playing for Scotland in Portugal in 1993 put Ally out of the game but he was back in season 1995/96 with twenty goals to his credit. Old friends, Celtic, regularly suffered at his hands - a McCoist 'hat-trick' in the Glasgow Cup Final of May 1986, allied to his trio of goals in the League Cup Final of 1984, meant that 'Super' became the first Rangers player to score three against them on two occasions.

The McCoist time at Ibrox ended with the beginning of the Advocaat era. Even in that last season, however, it was the player's attitude that lifted the team, late on, for one final push towards a possible 'double'. It was not to be.

Strikers with McCoist's predatory instincts are a rare breed. Be thankful he was a Ranger.

BRIAN LAUDRUP

BRIAN LAUDRUP, the 'Prince of Players', won the hearts of all 'Follow-Followers' right from the start. In his very first game for Rangers, against Motherwell at Ibrox (13.8.94), a magnificent mazy run the length of the field set up Duncan Ferguson's winning goal in the last minute.

After that, it was just a procession of highlights, with the Dane scoring 'Goals of the Season' , 'away' to Celtic (3-1, 3.10.94), Dundee United (3-0, 4.12.94) and Kilmarnock (2-1, 10.12.94). 'Player of the Year', without a doubt.

The following season, his winning goal against Celtic in the Scottish Cup semi final (2-1, 7.4.96) paved the way to a quite masterly 'Final' performance in the demolition of Hearts, when Rangers scored five to lift the trophy. Brian not only netted twice that day but created the other three as well.

The year of *'Nine-in-a-Row'* was, in many ways, also the year of Brian Laudrup. He was the maestro behind Rangers' two best shows of the season, at Tynecastle and Pittodrie in December, when both Hearts (3-0) and Aberdeen (4-1) were swept aside. More importantly, Celtic were beaten in four out of five league encounters, with the Dane claiming both goals in the 1-0 Parkhead triumphs of November and March. The latter spring clash virtually ended Celtic's slim hope of stopping Rangers' relentless pursuit of nine consecutive league titles. In May 1997, for the second time in three years, Laudrup was named 'Player of the Year' by the Scottish Football Writers' Association.

Although his last season at Ibrox, before heading south to Stamford Bridge and Chelsea, was not successful, his place in Ibrox legend was assured.

Brian Laudrup, a 'Prince of Players', indeed.

GEORGE YOUNG

ONE of the truly great Rangers captains, he won six League Championships, four Scottish Cups and two League Cups with the club from 1946 to 1957. George also won 53 Scottish caps and captained his country on no less than 48 occasions. His nickname 'Corky' referred to the habit he had of carrying a champagne cork in his pocket for luck.

RANGERS IN EUROPE

Part 1

THE FLEDGLING EUROPEAN CUP was only one year old in season 1956-57 when Rangers made their debut in European competition following the previous year's Scottish League Championship triumph.

After a first round 'bye', the Ibrox club were drawn against Nice of France. Level at three goals apiece following the 'home' and 'away' legs, the play-off was scheduled for Paris and the neutral venue of the Colombes Stadium. A crowd of some 15,000 saw Rangers dominate the first half with nothing to show for it. Nice eventually ran out 3-1 victors.

The following season, the European Cup beckoned once more and again Rangers faced opposition from the *'Auld Alliance'*. On this occasion, however, the French champions (now Saint Etienne) were defeated 4-3 for Scotland's hopefuls to progress to the next stage. Few teams would relish facing Italian giants, Milan, even in the 50s but this was now the task confronting Rangers. Neutrals feared the worst.

The outfit from the fashion capital of the world certainly turned on the style at Ibrox, finally winning 4-1 after netting four late goals in the space of some eleven minutes! The return leg was naturally only a formality as the home side added another two goals without reply.

There were no European nights at Ibrox the next year following failure to qualify but season 1959-60 saw the 'Light Blues' end the decade and swing into the sixties with a quite marvellous run to the semi final stage of the European Cup.

Following aggregate victories of 7-2 and 5-4 over Anderlecht (Belgium) and Red Star (Bratislava) of Czechoslovakia respectively, the Dutch champions, Sparta Rotterdam, lay in waiting at the quarter-final juncture. After a stunning 3-2 'away' victory, Rangers lost 1-0 in Glasgow. Arsenal Stadium in London was chosen for the play-off. Jimmy Millar and Sammy Baird (2) were the scorers as Rangers progressed on a 3-2 scoreline. Incidentally, Baird was the only Rangers player to have scored in the World Cup Finals before the 1990 competition!

Crushing defeats both 'away' (6-1) and 'home' (6-3) meant that the German club side, Eintracht Frankfurt, would face the mighty Real Madrid in that year's European Cup Final. Even now, some forty years on, people still talk of that astonishing game played at Hampden Park, when the Spaniards scored seven to lift the trophy.

Due to the outstanding success of this initial European tournament, the footballing authorities decided to create an additional event for cup winners - the European Cup Winners' Cup. Having lifted the Scottish Cup the previous season, Rangers would now represent Scotland in the inaugural competition. In doing so, the men from Govan would enter the history books and become, in May 1961, the first British club to reach the final of a European competition.

Along the way, the scalps of Ferencvaros (Hungary), Borussia Moenchengladbach (Germany) - an amazing 11-0 aggregate scoreline - and Wolverhampton Wanderers (England) were collected. However, Fiorentina of Italy were just too strong for the 'Gers in the final, winning both legs to secure an overall 4-1 triumph.

In many ways, this European success (and it was indeed success, even though an actual trophy still eluded them), came as no great surprise. As a playing unit, Rangers were a wonderful sight to behold and included in their ranks the talents of Eric Caldow, Harold Davis, Ian McMillan, Jimmy Millar, Ralph Brand and Davie Wilson, amongst others.

Also a certain slim young man had signed the previous close season from Raith Rovers for a record Scottish £17,500 fee. Touched by true genius, his place in Ibrox folklore is assured. The legend that is Jim Baxter is discussed elsewhere in this publication

Back in the European Cup for season 1961-62, Rangers encountered a bewildering series of adventures. Following a first-round victory over Monaco (a pleasant trip to Monte Carlo in early September was much appreciated by players and fans alike), a potentially hazardous journey to East Berlin to play East German champions, Vorwarts, was now on the cards.

In those days, Germany's major city was still divided and the Berlin Wall a very real and frightening reminder of the deep distrust that existed between East and West. John Le Carré territory, indeed!

A week after securing an important 2-1 November success in the 'fatherland', manager Scot Symon was forced to take his team to Malmo in Sweden for the corresponding 'home' fixture. This was simply because, due to the rampant paranoia of the times, the Vorwarts squad were refused visas to any NATO country, which obviously included Britain. Maybe it was just as well - imagine those dreaded Communists discovering the secrets of our mutton pies!

Malmo was chosen as venue for the game as neutral Sweden was not part of the North Atlantic Treaty Organisation, affording unhindered entry to the East Germans. Unfortunately, November fog meant that the game had to be abandoned - with Rangers 1-0 up. Amazingly, the match replay was scheduled for the following morning and resulted in a 4-1 victory for the Scots.

Due to the kick-off time being pre-noon, less than 1800 spectators watched the ninety minutes. An all-time-low attendance for Rangers in Europe! Belgian aces, Standard Liege, proved too strong in the quarter final and progressed 4-3 at the expense of our heroes.

The following season (1962-63) in the Cup Winners' Cup first round, Spanish outfit Seville were beaten 4-2. 'Lady Luck' then deserted and Tottenham Hotspur were drawn. Back in the early sixties, the team from White Hart Lane in London were thought by many to be one of the strongest club sides in Europe, with awesome players such as Jimmy Greaves, Dave Mackay and the tragic John White (he was killed by lightning in 1964) filling vital roles.

Once again, the gulf between the top teams in Scotland and England was rather wide - Spurs crushed Rangers 5-2 in the capital and then won 3-2 in Glasgow.

Unfortunately, sad times stay with the 'Light Blues' in Europe one year on, when, after qualification to the European Cup, Real Madrid appear on the horizon as opening adversaries. The very real fears are soon realised and, following a close 1-0 defeat at Ibrox, the Bernabeu Stadium in Spain's cultured city of Madrid is the setting for a masterly display of free-flowing football as the team in all-white score six goals without reply. Even Govan felt the shock waves that night!

It is said that you really only learn from defeat. In Rangers' case, this seemed to be true when next season's European campaign beckoned once more. After both legs, the score was tied at 5-5 with Yugoslavia's Red Star (Belgrade) in the first round of the European Cup. This was still the era when a play-off was required and so it was that the teams met again at Arsenal's Highbury Stadium in early November. Jim Forrest (2) and Ralph Brand scored to take the boys in blue through. In passing, it is worth noting that Jim Forrest scored fifty-seven goals in season 1964-65, a record still to this day.

Step forward the Austrian champions, Rapid Vienna. Rangers took a single goal advantage to the city that many people know only as the setting of the classic film, 'The Third Man'. Now it was the setting for a notable 2-0 victory. Jim Baxter was elegance personified that day but tragically his right leg was broken only minutes before the end. A cruel, cruel blow after such an outstanding performance.

As a young schoolboy in Glasgow, I vividly remember sneaking a transistor radio into class that afternoon, as the match was being broadcast live on the BBC, not exactly a common event in those days. The shock on hearing that my idol was being stretchered off was very quickly followed by the commentator's confirmation of a leg break. In that moment, the world seemed a harsh place, indeed.

Without Baxter, World Champions, Inter Milan, proved just too strong in the quarter final and advanced 3-2, eventually lifting the trophy.

In many ways, it was the end of an era at Ibrox. Jim Baxter was transferred to Sunderland at the end of the season and domestically Rangers would not hold the Championship for many years. In fact, until 1975.

There were no trips abroad (well, not officially) in the 1965-66 period but qualification was gained to the Cup Winners' Cup tournament one year on. Thrillingly, another final would beckon as the following teams fell by the wayside: Glentoran, Borussia Dortmund (the holders), Real Zaragoza (on the toss of a coin after a 2-2 draw) and Slavia Sofia in the 'semi'.

The final was scheduled to take place in Nuremberg against a relatively young Bayern Munich side that included such future stars as Müller, Roth, Maier and the famed Franz Beckenbauer. Expectations were high, with additional pressure from a Scottish public that had witnessed Celtic become the first British (and non-Latin) club side to lift the European Cup, only six days earlier.

Criticism is always easy with the benefit of hindsight. Manager Scot Symon had played Roger Hynd (mainly a defender) at centre-forward in the semi final.

Seemingly this was on the basis of a single reserve outing during which this nephew of Bill Shankly (yes - true!) scored four times whilst filling the position in an emergency. In fact, the fans' favourite, Alec Willoughby, had been dropped after netting sixteen goals in fourteen outings. The 'Follow-Follow' boys were, indeed, mystified.

Although Rangers suffered a 1-0 defeat after extra time, Hynd himself had missed a clear-cut chance from only six yards out during the regulation period. Maybe a more natural goalscorer would have converted. There was no doubting his commitment to the cause, however. It was revealed later that the big man had thrown away his loser's medal, perhaps not realising that it was identical to the winner's award he would, no doubt, have cherished.

The Inter-Cities Fairs Cup was the European objective in seasons 1967-68 and 1968-69. English clubs halted the progress of Rangers on both occasions, Leeds United at the quarter-final stage first of all (2-0) and then Newcastle United, one round on, the following year, with the same scoreline. It should be noted, however, that several impressive teams such as Dinamo Dresden (East Germany), Cologne (West Germany), Vojvodina (Yugoslavia) and Atletico Bilbao (Spain) fell to the Scots prior to their own demise.

The next year's sojourn in the Cup Winners' Cup is chiefly remembered for the fact that, after being outplayed by the Poles of Gornik Zabrze over two legs (6-2 aggregate), manager David White was sacked. He had filled the post for barely two years.

Part 2

A NEW DECADE ... but little else had changed on foreign shores, as the club exited in the opening round of the Fairs Cup of 1970-71 to Bayern Munich, despite being the better of the two teams both 'home' and 'away'. Change was coming, though - and in a few month's time, Rangers would leave some of the best teams in Europe dead and buried to finally realise the ultimate goal of European glory.

And so it came to pass that season 1971-72 was a landmark one in the history of the club .... but the path to immortality was an exacting one.

Tommy McLean celebrates Rangers' goal against Bayern Munich at Ibrox in the semi final of the Cup Winners' Cup, April 1972.

Autumnal Glasgow waited for French side Rennes after a 1-1 draw in the first round, first leg tie. Alex MacDonald's goal (the only one of the night) saw Rangers progress to face one of the top Portuguese clubs, Sporting Lisbon, in the October/November of 1971. All was going according to plan initially, as the 'Light Blues' swept into a commanding 3-0 lead at the interval in the opening ninety minutes. But two second-half goals from Chic and Gomez ensured that the return match would be no formality for John Greig's men.

Sixty thousand fans witnessed a memorable night in Lisbon as the 'home' side just managed to win by the same scoreline of 3-2 (their third goal coming just seven minutes before the final whistle) for an aggregate 5-5 result. Both teams netted again in extra time. Although still level at six goals apiece, Rangers would go through on the 'away goals' ruling. Or so they thought ....

Maier Saves from Colin Stein in the semi final of the European Cup Winners' Cup, Ibrox, April 1972.

The referee ruled that a 'penalty shoot-out' would now take place to decide the winners. Rangers lost on penalties. Manager Willie Waddell, however, sought out the UEFA representative on duty and it was eventually confirmed that the Scots had, indeed, qualified on the 'away goals' scenario. Joy mingled with tears, nonetheless, as centre-half, Ronnie McKinnon, had suffered a double fracture of his right leg during the game.

Now it was Torino of Italy in the quarter final. Following a fine 1-1 draw abroad, Alex MacDonald's solitary goal (a re-run of the first round) at Ibrox was enough to take Rangers through to the frightening prospect of Bayern Munich next.

Frightening? Yes, indeed, as this Bayern side included Roth, Höeness, Breitner, Maier, Müller and Beckenbauer. All six would be part of the West German national outfit which would win the European Championship in Brussels (defeating USSR 3-0) some weeks later.

Again, the continent brought out the best in the boys from Govan, as a 1-1 draw in Germany confirmed. A crowd of eighty thousand viewed an amazing start at Ibrox as Sandy Jardine scored in the very first minute of the second leg. Young Derek Parlane added a second and Rangers were through to their third

Alex MacDonald surrounded by Moscow Dynamo players in the European Cup Winners' Cup Final of 1972.

European final on a 2-0 scoreline. Surely they would not fail again ....

May 24th 1972, the Nou Camp Stadium, Barcelona - the date and venue for the European Cup Winners' Cup Final. In reaching the final, Moscow Dynamo had become the first Russian side ever to make this stage of any European competition.

Colin Stein opened the scoring in twenty-four minutes to the delight of some twenty thousand 'Follow-Followers' in the crowd. Only four minutes of the second half had been played when Willie Johnston grabbed his second goal of the night (his first being a header just prior to the interval) following a typical Peter

Rangers fans celebrate on the pitch at the end of the European Cup Winners' Cup Final, Barcelona, 1972.

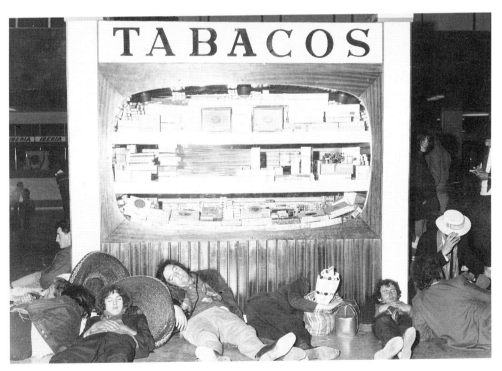

Waiting for the flight home.

McCloy kick-out deep into the opposition area to give Rangers a commanding 3-0 advantage. Despite two Russian replies, a 3-2 victory had been gloriously recorded for prosperity. Finally, silverware of a non-Scottish variety would be carried up that famous marble stairway to the Trophy Room.

Maybe inevitably, there was a down side. Over-reactive Spanish riot police did not take kindly to Rangers fans invading the park at the sound of the final whistle and many ugly scenes ensued. UEFA imposed a severe penalty - the club was banned from all official European competition for two full seasons.

Captain John Greig holds aloft the European Cup Winners' Cup.

Dutch masters, Ajax, were entertained the following season in the first-ever European Super Cup. This was a new trophy decided over two 'friendly' matches between the winners of the previous season's major continental awards, the European Cup and the Cup Winners' Cup. Ajax proved far too strong at this level and secured 3-1 and 3-2 victories.

Some good did come from this, though, as, partly due to the good behaviour of Scottish fans at the game in Amsterdam, Rangers' ban in Europe was reduced on appeal to just one year.

September 1974 and the lads were back - in Turkey! The obscure team of

Ankaragucu were soundly beaten, with Rangers taking six goals (and losing none) off the swarthy gentlemen before having to face the teutonic might of Borussia Moenchengladbach. Back in 1960, the Germans had suffered an 11-0 humiliation but times had changed. On this occasion, a 3-0 'home' victory was enough to see them through, even though they lost out to the odd goal in five in Glasgow.

At long last Rangers were back in the fold of the European Cup following their domestic triumph of 1975. An early exit at the hands of Saint Etienne of France followed progress past Ireland's Bohemians (Dublin) in the first round. It was of little consolation that the Gauls would make it all the way to that year's final at Hampden Park, only to lose somewhat unluckily to Bayern Munich, the holders.

The fans were presented with even less joy next season when they had to suffer an embarrassing first-round exit at the hands of FC Zurich of Switzerland. Cuckoo clocks were sounding everywhere!

Rangers v Juventus, European Cup, September 1978.

Season 1977-78 and Rangers eased past Young Boys (Switzerland - again) at the opening stage of the Cup Winners' Cup, even though Derek Johnstone was sent off in the second ('away') leg. This was, in fact, a repeat of the same offence in Switzerland the previous year. Dutch side Twente Enschede stopped any further advancement with a 3-0 aggregate scoreline.

In John Greig's first season as manager the next year, Rangers were an absolute revelation in Europe. The mighty Juventus (with nine World Cup stars in their line-up) were drawn first of all in the European Cup. A fine defensive display in the Stadio Communale limited the Italians to a single-goal advantage, which was overturned at Ibrox in a 2-0 triumph.

PSV Eindhoven had never lost a home European tie - ever. After a goalless opening game in Glasgow, they were clear favourites on their own patch. What followed was one of Rangers' greatest ever victories on foreign soil. After going behind twice in the game, Bobby Russell clinched victory with a 3-2 scoreline barely three minutes before the end.

The European Cup had become a very real possibility in the eyes of both players and fans. Sadly, it was not to be. A Rangers selection at the quarter-final stage, depleted due to injuries, lost out 2-1 on aggregate to Cologne. Another dream was gone.

The Cup Winners' Cup campaign of 1979 was ended by the magic of Mario Kempes of Valencia. Although a 1-1 'away' draw raised hopes, the Spaniards' class shone through in Scotland for a 3-1 result, with Kempes scoring a superb double. His team went on to win the tournament.

Two years on in 1981, Rangers' return to the European fray did not last long and the Czech army side of Dukla Prague completed a 4-2 winning scoreline. There was certainly improvement the following season but after victory over Borussia Dortmund in the UEFA Cup first round, another German side destroyed Rangers 5-0 in Cologne.

At least season 1983-84 raised some cheer in Europe: a Scottish record win of 18-0 over Malta's Valletta. The first leg on the Mediterranean island was witness to an 8-0 victory and a record four goals from - wait for it - Dave McPherson! FC Porto of Portugal halted any further steps in the Cup Winners' Cup that year on the 'away goals' ruling.

The UEFA Cup campaign of the next period brought Inter Milan to Glasgow, bringing with them a three-goal lead acquired in Italy. A night of great character and passion to ensure an admirable 3-1 outcome in Glasgow was not quite enough for Rangers. So near and yet so far.

Highs and lows always seem to follow in quick succession and so it was as the club exited the UEFA Cup again the following year. No glory here, however, as the lowly Spanish team, Atletico Osasuna, advanced with a 2-1 scoreline. Times were changing again that season, nevertheless, and very soon there would be only one name on everyone's lips as Rangers entered a new era.

Graeme James Souness arrived as player-manager in April 1986. Scottish football would never be the same again. His first European campaign in charge (in the UEFA Cup) resulted in victories over Ilves of Finland and Boavista of Portugal. After a 1-1 draw at Ibrox and a 0-0 scoreline in Germany, Borussia Moencheneladbach progressed at Rangers' expense. Stuart Munro and Davie Cooper had both been dismissed in controversial circumstances during the 'away' fixture.

As champions, the European Cup beckoned in season 1987-88. The 'Light Blues' did not disappoint. At this time, Dynamo Kiev were considered by those in the know to be one of the top club sides in the world. They also formed the nucleus of the Soviet national team. They were Rangers' first round targets. A first-leg single goal deficit was overturned at Ibrox by a 2-0 victory. Still today, Rangers fans speak of the incredible atmosphere and noise created by the supporters that night.

A 4-2 aggregate win over Gornik Zabrze and Souness' men were into the last eight. The loss of captain Terry Butcher (with a broken leg) prior to the quarter-final ties was a major blow and so it proved, as the powerful Steaua Bucharest team from Rumania knocked out Rangers, just 3-2 overall.

This was to be the only time that the team would reach the last eight in Europe during the Souness era. Emulation of the manager's domestic success was never realised.

Next year's UEFA Cup began well. After beating GKS Katowice 1-0 at 'home', a visit to Poland secured an excellent 4-2 victory, with Terry Butcher scoring twice. Old rivals, Cologne, were next but for the third successive time, Rangers failed to score in the famous cathedral city. The Germans progressed 3-1.

Season 1989-90 brought early elimination at the hands of the redoubtable Bayern Munich in the European Cup. The next year was Souness' last in charge

- Rangers lost out (aggregate 4-1) to the eventual winners of the Champions' Cup, Red Star Belgrade.

There was little improvement in Walter Smith's first season at the helm. Although somewhat unfortunate, the club lost out on the 'away goals' ruling to Sparta Prague.

Season 1992-93 was an altogether different 'European Cup' story. Following an aggregate 3-0 victory over Lyngby of Denmark, English champions, Leeds United, were drawn in the second round.

Despite losing a goal in the first minute at Ibrox, Rangers still won 2-1 on the night. Needless to say, the English media had, by this time, written off the 'Light Blues' chances of progressing further in the tournament - Leeds would destroy them in the second leg of this *'Battle of Britain'*. Suffice to say that Rangers wrote another glorious chapter in their history, winning 2-1 again with goals from the striking partnership of Hateley and McCoist.

The Ibrox club then joined Marseille, CSKA Moscow and FC Brugge of Belgium in the 'Group A' section before eventually losing out narrowly to the French champions. (Marseille, in fact, won the European Cup that year). Rangers had been unbeaten in all six games in the section but four drawn games proved too costly. Even without a defeat, the team exited.

Following such a glorious campaign (and further League flags in Scotland), Rangers were disappointingly eliminated at the first stage for the next two years, losing to Levski Sofia (on 'away' goals after a 4-4 aggregate) and AEK Athens of Greece, with defeats in both legs.

In 1995, a 1-0 victory over Anorthosis Famagusta of Cyprus, although hardly impressive, ensured qualification into the lucrative *'Champions' League'*. On this occasion, Steaua Bucharest, Borussia Dortmund and the mighty Juventus were bedfellows.

Creditable drawn efforts in three games were cancelled out by 'home' and 'away' defeats at the hands of Juventus (4-0 and 4-1 respectively).

Certainly season 1996-97 began well enough when Rangers, after a 3-1 'home' result against Vladikavkaz, travelled to the Soviet Republic and thrashed the Russian champions 7-2 on their own ground. There now seemed a real chance of progress especially when it was confirmed that Grasshoppers

(Switzerland), Auxerre (France) and Ajax (Holland) would be in the same *'Champions' League'* group.

Hopes were soon dashed, however, when Grasshoppers won 3-0 in Zurich in the first game. Rangers would eventually lose every tie bar one in the section.

Walter Smith's final year in charge (1997-98) was to prove another disappointment in Europe. Following a 4-1 aggregate defeat by IFK Gothenburg of Sweden in the second qualifying round, a new ruling ensured that the club gained automatic entry into round one of the UEFA Cup. The French side, RC Strasbourg, won both legs by the same 2-1 scoreline.

The European scene had changed dramatically since Rangers met Nice way back in 1956. The club had achieved greatness in winning the Cup Winners' Cup in 1972 but the ultimate goal, the 'Holy Grail' of the European Cup, still eluded them.

EUROPEAN CUP

		Home	Away	Agg
1956-57				
Round 1	Nice	2-1	1-2	3-3
Rangers lost the play-off 1-3				
1957-58				
Preliminary	St. Etienne	3-1	1-2	4-3
Round 1	AC Milan	1-4	0-2	1-6
1959-60				
Qualifier	Anderlecht	5-2	2-0	4-3
Round 1	Red Star Bratislava	4-3	1-1	5-4
Quarter Final	Sparta Rotterdam	0-1	3-2	3-3
Rangers won the play-off 3-2				
Semi Final	Eintracht Frankfurt	3-6	1-6	4-12
1961-62				
Preliminary	Monaco	3-2	3-2	6-4
Round 1	Vorwaerts Berlin	4-1	2-1	6-2
Quarter Final	Standard Liege	2-0	1-4	3-4
1963-64				
Preliminary	Real Madrid	0-1	0-6	0-7
1964-65				
Preliminary	Red Star Belgrade	3-1	2-4	5-5
Rangers won the play-off 3-1				
Round 1	Rapid Vienna	1-0	2-0	3-0
Quarter Final	Inter Milan	1-0	1-3	2-3
1975-76				
Round 1	Bohemians	4-1	1-1	5-2
Round 2	St. Etienne	1-2	0-2	1-4
1976-77				
Round 1	Zurich	1-1	0-1	1-2
1978-79				
Round 1	Juventus	2-0	0-1	2-1
Round 2	PSV Eindhoven	0-0	3-2	3-2
Quarter Final	Cologne	1-1	0-1	1-2
1987-88				
Round 1	Dynamo Kiev	2-0	0-1	2-1
Round 2	Gornik Zabrze	3-1	1-1	4-2
Quarter Final	Steaua Bucharest	2-1	0-2	2-3
1989-90				
Round 1	Bayern Munich	1-3	0-0	1-3

		Home	Away	Agg
1990-91				
Round 1	Valletta	6-0	4-0	10-0
Round 2	Red Star Belgrade	1-1	0-3	1-4
1991-92				
Round 1	Sparta Prague	2-1	0-1	2-2
Rangers lost on 'away goals' rule				
1992-93				
Round 1	Lyngby	2-0	1-0	3-0
Round 2	Leeds United	2-1	2-1	4-2
Group A	Marseille	2-2	-	-
Group A	CSKA Moscow	-	1-0	-
Group A	FC Brugge	-	1-1	-
Group A	FC Brugge	2-1	-	-
Group A	Marseille	-	1-1	-
Group A	CSKA Moscow	0-0	-	-
1993-94				
Round 1	Levski Sofia	3-2	1-2	4-4
Rangers lost on 'away goals' rule				
1994-95				
Preliminary	AEK Athens	0-1	0-2	0-3
1995-96				
Preliminary	Anorthosis Famagusta	1-0	0-0	1-0
Group A	Steaua Bucharest	-	0-1	-
Group A	Borussia Dortmund	2-2	-	-
Group A	Juventus	-	1-4	-
Group A	Juventus	0-4	-	-
Group A	Steaua Bucharest	1-1	-	-
Group A	Borussia Dortmund	-	2-2	-
1996-97				
Preliminary	Vladikavkaz	3-1	7-2	10-3
Group A	Grasshoppers	-	0-3	-
Group A	Auxerre	1-2	-	-
Group A	Ajax	-	1-4	-
Group A	Ajax	0-1	-	-
Group A	Grasshoppers	2-1	-	-
Group A	Auxerre	-	1-2	-
1997-98				
Qualifier 1	GI Gotu	6-0	5-0	11-0
Qualifier 2	IFK Gothenberg	1-1	0-3	1-4

UEFA CUP

		Home	Away	Agg
1967-68				
Round 1	Dynamo Dresden	2-1	1-1	3-2
Round 2	Cologne	3-0	1-3	4-3
Round 3	'Bye'			
Quarter Final	Leeds United	0-0	0-2	0-2
1968-69				
Round 1	Vojvodina	2-0	0-1	2-1
Round 2	Dundalk	6-1	3-0	9-1
Round 3	DWS Amsterdam	2-1	2-0	4-1
Quarter Final	Atletico Bilbao	4-1	0-2	4-3
Semi Final	Newcastle United	0-0	0-2	0-2
1970-71				
Round 1	Bayern Munich	1-1	0-1	1-2
1982-83				
Round 1	Borussia Dortmund	2-0	0-0	2-0
Round 2	Cologne	2-1	0-5	2-6
1984-85				
Round 1	Bohemians	2-0	2-3	4-3
Round 2	Inter Milan	3-1	0-3	3-4
1985-86				
Round 1	Osasuna	1-0	0-2	1-2
1986-87				
Round 1	Ilves Tampere	4-0	0-2	4-2
Round 2	Boavista	2-1	1-0	3-1
Round 3	B. Moenchengladbach	1-1	0-0	1-1
Rangers lost on 'away goals' rule				
1988-89				
Round 1	Katowice	1-0	4-2	5-2
Round 2	Cologne	1-1	0-2	1-3
1997-98				
Round 1	RC Strasbourg	1-2	1-2	2-4

EUROPEAN CUP WINNERS' CUP

		Home	Away	Agg
1960-61				
Qualifier	Ferencvaros	4-2	1-2	5-4
Quarter Final	B. Moenchengladbach	8-0	3-0	11-0
Semi Final	Wolves	2-0	1-1	3-1
Final	Fiorentina	0-2	1-2	1-4
1962-63				
Round 1	Seville	4-0	0-2	4-2
Round 2	Tottenham Hotspur	2-3	2-5	4-8
1966-67				
Round 1	Glentoran	4-0	1-1	5-1
Round 2	Borussia Dortmund	2-1	0-0	2-1
Quarter Final	Real Zaragoza	2-0	0-2	2-2
Rangers won on toss of coin				
Semi Final	Slavia Sofia	1-0	1-0	2-0
Final	Bayern Munich	-	-	0-1
1969-70				
Round 1	Steaua Bucharest	2-0	0-0	2-0
Round 2	Gornik Zabrze	1-3	1-3	2-6
1971-72				
Round 1	Rennes	1-0	1-1	2-1
Round 2	Sporting Lisbon	3-2	3-4	6-6
Rangers won on 'away goals' rule				
Quarter Final	Torino	1-0	1-1	2-1
Semi Final	Bayern Munich	2-0	1-1	3-1
Final	Moscow Dynamo	-	-	3-2
1973-74				
Round 1	Ankaragucu	4-0	2-0	6-0
Round 2	B. Moenchengladbach	3-2	0-3	3-5
1977-78				
Preliminary	Young Boys Berne	1-0	2-2	3-2
Round 1	Twente Enschede	0-0	0-3	0-3
1979-80				
Preliminary	Lillestrom	1-0	2-0	3-0
Round 1	Fortuna Düsseldorf	2-1	0-0	2-1
Round 2	Valencia	1-3	1-1	2-4
1981-82				
Round 1	Dukla Prague	2-1	0-3	2-4
1983-84				
Round 1	Valletta	10-0	8-0	18-0
Round 2	Porto	2-1	0-1	2-2
Rangers lost on 'away goals' rule				

SCOTTISH LEAGUE CUP
WINNING SEASONS

1946-47

Rangers won the first-ever League Cup competition defeating Aberdeen 4-0 in the final, with goals from Jimmy Duncanson (2), Torry Gillick and Billy Williamson. On final day, the weather was so bad that only (!) 82,684 spectators turned up, despite 134,000 tickets being sold.

Section	St. Mirren	4-0, 4-0
Section	Queen's Park	4-2, 1-0
Section	Morton	3-0, 2-0
Quarter Final	Dundee United	2-1, 1-1
Semi Final	Hibernian	3-1
Final	Aberdeen	4-0

1948-49

An amazing 105,000 fans watched Rangers beat Celtic 2-1 in the 'Section' stage early on this season. Division 'B' side, Raith Rovers, lost 2-0 in the final, with Torry Gillick and Willie Paton on the scoresheet.

Section	Clyde	1-1, 3-1
Section	Hibernian	0-0, 1-0
Section	Celtic	1-3, 2-1
Quarter Final	St. Mirren	1-0
Semi Final	Dundee	4-1
Final	Raith Rovers	2-0

1960-61

Ralph Brand, who favoured the 'new' lightweight continental boots, was one of the great Rangers goalscorers and formed a deadly partnership with Jimmy Millar in the early sixties. Dismissed as 'just a poacher' he was never on the losing side in seven finals, scoring six goals.

Both Brand and Alex Scott netted in this season's 2-0 victory over Kilmarnock.

Section	Partick Thistle	3-1, 4-1
Section	Third Lanark	1-2, 3-2
Section	Celtic	2-3, 2-1
Quarter Final	Dundee	1-0, 4-3
Semi Final	Queen of the South	7-0
Final	Kilmarnock	2-0

1961-62
Hearts were the better of the teams in the first 'final' game, which was drawn 1-1. However, in the December replay, Rangers were streets ahead, with Millar, Brand and Ian McMillan all scoring.

Section	Third Lanark	2-0, 5-0
Section	Dundee	4-2, 1-1
Section	Airdrieonians	2-1, 4-1
Quarter Final	East Fife	3-1, 3-1
Semi Final	St. Johnstone	3-2
Final	Hearts	1-1, 3-1

1963-64
Second Division Morton were crushed 5-0 before nearly 106,000 witnesses. Cousins Jim Forrest and Alec Willoughby were the day's heroes, claiming all five between them with Jim netting four to establish a Cup Final record. The striker had earlier put two past Celtic in the 3-0 Parkhead triumph.

Section	Celtic	3-0, 3-0
Section	Queen of the South	5-2, 5-2
Section	Kilmarnock	4-1, 2-2
Quarter Final	East Fife	1-1, 2-0
Semi Final	Berwick Rangers	3-1
Final	Morton	5-0

1964-65
Jim Forrest was again the man of the hour, striking twice against Celtic in the final as Rangers retained the trophy.

Section	Aberdeen	4-0, 4-3
Section	St. Mirren	0-0, 6-2
Section	St. Johnstone	9-1, 3-1
Quarter Final	Dunfermline Ath.	3-0, 2-2
Semi Final	Dundee United	2-1
Final	Celtic	2-1

1970-71
Victory over Celtic again, with sixteen-year-old Derek Johnstone's legendary headed goal. The club's first major trophy in four years.

Section	Dunfermline	4-1, 6-0
Section	Motherwell	2-0, 2-0
Section	Morton	0-0, 2-0
Quarter Final	Hibernian	3-1, 3-1
Semi Final	Cowdenbeath	2-0
Final	Celtic	1-0

1975-76

John Greig lifted the trophy for the first time as captain, following Alex MacDonald's famous diving header.

Section	Airdrieonians	6-1, 2-1
Section	Clyde	1-0, 6-0
Section	Motherwell	1-1, 2-2
Quarter Final	Queen of the South	1-0, 2-2
Semi Final	Montrose	5-1
Final	Celtic	1-0

1977-78

Extra time was required when the 'Old Firm' crossed swords again in March 1978. Both Davie Cooper and Gordon Smith were on target, thus ensuring part one of another 'treble' celebration.

Round 2	St. Johnstone	3-1, 3-0
Round 3	Aberdeen	6-1, 1-3
Quarter Final	Dunfermline Ath.	3-1, 3-1
Semi Final	Forfar Athletic	5-2
Final	Celtic	5-2

1978-79

In a dramatic final confrontation, the 'Light Blues' came from behind, scoring twice in the last thirteen minutes to snatch the prize from Aberdeen. Alex MacDonald and centre-half, Colin Jackson (in the dying seconds of the regulation period), scored for Rangers to give John Greig his first major trophy as manager.

Round 1	Albion Rovers	3-0, 1-0
Round 2	Forfar Athletic	3-0, 4-1
Round 3	St. Mirren	3-2, 0-0
Quarter Final	Arbroath	1-0, 2-1
Semi Final	Celtic	3-2
Final	Aberdeen	2-1

1981-82

Two dramatic strikes from Davie Cooper and Ian Redford (both from some twenty yards), in the last fifteen minutes, cancelled out Dundee United's earlier goal in the late-November final.

Section	Morton	1-1, 1-0
Section	Dundee	4-1, 2-1
Section	Raith Rovers	8-1, 3-1
Quarter Final	Brechin City	4-0, 1-0
Semi Final	St. Mirren	2-2, 2-1
Final	Dundee United	2-1

1983-84

In a thrilling contest, it was an Ally McCoist 'hat-trick' against old rivals, Celtic, that enabled Rangers to lift the trophy (after extra-time) for a record twelfth time. 'Super' was top scorer that year, with twenty-two domestic goals to his credit.

Round 2	Queen of the South	4-0, 4-1
Section	Clydebank	4-0, 3-0
Section	Hearts	3-0, 2-0
Section	St. Mirren	5-0, 1-0
Semi Final	Dundee United	1-1, 2-0
Final	Celtic	3-2

1984-85

A solitary Iain Ferguson goal on a miserably wet day and the League Cup was Ibrox-bound. At the start of that season, Ferguson had signed from Dundee, whose near neighbours, United, faced Rangers in the final.

Round 2	Falkirk	1-0
Round 3	Raith Rovers	4-0
Quarter Final	Cowdenbeath	3-1
Semi Final	Meadowbank	4-0, 1-1
Final	Dundee United	1-0

1986-87

Ian Durrant and Davie Cooper (from the penalty spot) gave Graeme Souness his first major trophy as Rangers boss. Especially pleasing was the fact that 'Old Firm' rivals, Celtic, were the 2-1 victims.

Round 2	Stenhousemuir	4-1
Round 3	East Fife	0-0
Rangers won on penalties		
Quarter Final	Dundee	3-1
Semi Final	Dundee United	2-1
Final	Celtic	2-1

1987-88

One of the great finals of modern times. After Aberdeen opened the scoring, goals from Davie Cooper (a really quite ferocious free-kick) and Ian Durrant gave Rangers the lead. The team from the north then scored twice, late on, before Robert Fleck's dramatic late, late equaliser. With no further scoring in extra time, it was all down to penalties. Remember Ian Durrant, arms aloft in victory 'V' celebration, after he had netted the decisive kick?

Round 2	Stirling Albion	2-1
Round 3	Dunfermline Ath.	4-1
Quarter Final	Hearts	4-1
Semi Final	Motherwell	3-1
Final	Aberdeen	3-3
Rangers won 5-3 on penalties		

1988-89

Another memorable game against Aberdeen. Ally McCoist's last-minute goal (his second of the day) ensured that the trophy was Govan-bound for the third successive year. The previous year's hero, Ian Durrant, was missing, injured after that shocking Pittodrie tackle in October's league match.

Round 2	Clyde	3-0
Round 3	Clydebank	6-0
Quarter Final	Dundee	4-1
Semi Final	Hearts	3-0
Final	Aberdeen	3-2

1990-91

A goal of a start was not enough for Celtic, thanks to strikes from Mark Walters and Richard Gough. The final went into extra time for the second successive year before Gough's winner.

Round 2	East Stirling	5-0
Round 3	Kilmarnock	1-0
Quarter Final	Raith Rovers	6-2
Semi Final	Aberdeen	1-0
Final	Celtic	2-1

1992-93

In what was to be another 'treble' season, Aberdeen would perish in both the Scottish and League Cup Finals. The latter game required extra time again for Rangers to record a 2-1 triumph.

Round 2	Dumbarton	5-0
Round 3	Stranraer	5-0
Quarter Final	Dundee United	3-2
Semi Final	St. Johnstone	3-1
Final	Aberdeen	2-1

1993-94

Rangers and Hibs met in the final for the first time ever, after both Aberdeen and Celtic had been disposed of along the way. 'A Kind of Magic' is really the only way to describe substitute Ally's legendary winner.

Round 2	Dumbarton	1-0
Round 3	Dunfermline Ath.	2-0
Quarter Final	Aberdeen	2-1
Semi Final	Celtic	1-0
Final	Hibernian	2-1

1996-97

On a cold, cold November day, the genius of Paul Gascoigne was all that separated the teams. Two sublime moments, in a three-minute period, decided the trophy's ultimate destination. The record books again welcomed 'Super Ally' (Rangers' other scorer of two that day) as he had now totalled eight goals in League Cup Finals. Coincidentally, the legend had also equalled the great Jim Forrest's Rangers record of fifty goals in this competition.

Round 2	Clydebank	3-0
Round 3	Ayr United	3-1
Quarter Final	Hibernian	4-0
Semi Final	Dunfermline Ath.	6-1
Final	Hearts	4-3

THE SCOTTISH CUP
WINNING SEASONS

1893-94

After 21 years of trying, Rangers first-ever Scottish Cup was won by beating Celtic 3-1 in the final, played in February that season. For the record, McCreadie, Barker and McPherson were the scorers.

Round 1	Cowlairs	8-0
Round 2	Leith Athletic	2-0
Quarter Final	Clyde	5-0
Semi Final	Queen's Park	1-1, 3-1
Final	Celtic	3-1

1896-97

Both the 'Glasgow' and 'Charity' Cups joined the 'Scottish' at Ibrox this year. Dumbarton were beaten 5-1 in the main final. Rangers became known as the 'Three Cup Team'.

Round 1	Partick Thistle	4-2
Round 2	Hibernian	3-0
Quarter Final	Dundee	4-0
Semi Final	Morton	7-2
Final	Dumbarton	5-1

1897-98

The Scottish Cup was retained with a 2-0 win over Kilmarnock. Sixteen of the twenty-two players involved, hailed from Ayrshire. One of Rangers scorers, R. C. Hamilton, had actually sat an exam at Glasgow University earlier that day!

Round 1	Polton Vale	8-0
Round 2	Cartvale	12-0
Quarter Final	Queen's Park	3-1
Semi Final	Third Lanark	1-1, 2-2, 2-0
Final	Kilmarnock	2-0

1902-03

After two drawn games against Hearts in the final, gate prices were halved to sixpence (2½p) for the second replay One of the most popular players, Finlay Speedie, was the Ally McCoist of this era. In 1906, Newcastle purchased his services for the princely sum of £600, which was quite a fee in those days.

Round 1	Auchterarder Thistle	7-0
Round 2	Kilmarnock	4-0
Quarter Final	Celtic	3-0
Semi Final	Stenhousemuir	4-1
Final	Hearts	1-1, 0-0, 2-0

1927-28

Twenty-five years on and a record crowd of over 118,000 witnessed one of the most acclaimed victories over Celtic. First-half dominance by the Parkhead men had kept Rangers on the defensive and it was mainly the brilliance of goalkeeper, Tom Hamilton, that ensured the 'Light Blues' were still level at the interval. Famously, a much rejuvenated Ibrox crew scored four in the second half. David Meiklejohn's penalty was followed by goals from Bob McPhail and Sandy Archibald (2). Cup holders, Celtic, were well beaten.

Round 1	East Stirlingshire	6-0
Round 2	Cowdenbeath	4-2
Round 3	King's Park	3-1
Quarter Final	Albion Rovers	1-0
Semi Final	Hibernian	3-0
Final	Celtic	4-0

1929-30

After defeating Partick Thistle 2-1 in the replayed final, the Scottish Cup joined the League Championship, the Glasgow Cup, the Glasgow Charity Cup, the Second Eleven Cup and the Scottish Alliance (the Reserve League Championship) at Ibrox.

The club had won every competition they were eligible to enter - a world record, since unequalled.

Round 1	Queen's Park	1-0
Round 2	Cowdenbeath	2-2, 3-0
Round 3	Motherwell	5-2
Quarter Final	Montrose	3-0
Semi Final	Hearts	4-1
Final	Partick Thistle	0-0, 2-1

1931-32

Another final replay, this time with Kilmarnock, who suffered a 3-0 defeat. Motherwell, who would lift the League Championship trophy, were crushed 5-2 in the third round.

Round 1	Brechin City	8-2
Round 2	Raith Rovers	5-0
Round 3	Hearts	1-0
Quarter Final	Motherwell	2-0
Semi Final	Hamilton	5-2
Final	Kilmarnock	1-1, 3-0

1933-34

The hero of the day was Billy Nicholson, who scored twice in his team's comfortable 5-0 victory over St. Mirren. In the first round tie against Blairgowrie, Jimmy Fleming scored nine goals - a club record.

Round 1	Blairgowrie	14-2
Round 2	Third Lanark	3-0
Round 3	Hearts	0-0, 2-1
Quarter Final	Aberdeen	1-0
Semi Final	St. Johnstone	1-0
Final	St. Mirren	5-0

1934-35

Hamilton Accies were the beaten team (2-1) this year in the final, a week after Rangers had won the Championship at Pittodrie with a 3-1 victory.

Round 1	Cowdenbeath	3-1
Round 2	Third Lanark	2-0
Round 3	St. Mirren	1-0
Quarter Final	Motherwell	4-1
Semi Final	Hearts	1-1, 2-0
Final	Hamilton	2-1

1935-36

A trio of successive cup wins was completed when Bob McPhail scored the only goal of the game against Third Lanark in just ninety seconds. This gave the Ibrox legend his seventh winner's medal. Quite a tally.

Round 1	East Fife	3-1
Round 2	Albion Rovers	3-1
Round 3	St. Mirren	2-1
Quarter Final	Aberdeen	1-0
Semi Final	Clyde	3-0
Final	Third Lanark	1-0

1947-48

The post-war demand for football saw attendances soar. An unbelievable crowd of 143,570 watched the semi final with Hibernian - a British record. A solitary Willie Thornton goal, from a Willie Waddell cross, decided the issue. Rangers met Morton in the final and won by a Billy Williamson headed goal in extra time after a replay. Billy had scored on his first-ever Scottish Cup appearance for the club. Also, another record had been set, as an amazing combined total of 261,151 spectators watched the two games.

Round 1	Stranraer	1-0
Round 2	Leith Athletic	4-0
Round 3	Partick Thistle	3-0
Quarter Final	East Fife	1-0
Semi Final	Hibernian	1-0
Final	Morton	1-1, 1-0

1948-49

Clyde were the final victims as Rangers recorded a 4-1 scoreline to achieve Scottish football's first ever 'treble' of League Championship, League Cup and Scottish Cup. Yet again, Billy Williamson was making his first Scottish Cup appearance of the season and - yes - yet again he scored!

Round 1	Elgin City	6-1
Round 2	Motherwell	3-0
Round 3	'Bye'	
Quarter Final	Partick Thistle	4-0
Semi Final	East Fife	3-0
Final	Clyde	4-1

1949-50

Willie Thornton was quite outstanding as he netted twice in the 3-0 victory over East Fife. In fact, a third strike had been disallowed (for offside), thus denying him the opportunity to become the first-ever Rangers player to score a 'hat-trick' in the final.

Yet another trio of triumphs to follow the threesome of 1934, 1935 and 1936.

Round 1	Motherwell	4-2
Round 2	Cowdenbeath	8-0
Round 3	'Bye'	
Quarter Final	Raith Rovers	1-1, 1-1, 2-0
Semi Final	Queen of the South	1-1, 3-0
Final	East Fife	3-0

1952-53

The year of a drama-filled final against Aberdeen. Captain George 'Corky' Young ended up in goal for eighteen minutes prior to half time after George Niven had been stretchered off with a head injury. Returning for the second period swathed in bandages, the 'keeper was outstanding. Ending in a 1-1 draw, Rangers sealed victory with a single Billy Simpson strike in the replay.

Round 1	Arbroath	4-0
Round 2	Dundee	2-0
Round 3	Morton	4-1
Quarter Final	Celtic	2-0
Semi Final	Hearts	2-1
Final	Aberdeen	1-1, 1-0

1959-60

After disposing of Celtic 4-1 in the semi-final replay (Jimmy Millar and David Wilson notching two each), Rangers' 15th Scottish Cup victory was accomplished with a 2-0 scoreline over Kilmarnock with Jimmy Millar again scoring twice.

Round 1	Berwick Rangers	3-1
Round 2	Arbroath	2-0
Round 3	Stenhousemuir	3-0
Quarter Final	Hibernian	3-2
Semi Final	Celtic	1-1, 4-1
Final	Kilmarnock	2-0

1961-62

The deadly left-wing partnership of Ralph Brand and Davie Wilson was renowned throughout the land. Both scored as St. Mirren lost 2-0.

Round 1	Falkirk	2-1
Round 2	Arbroath	6-0
Round 3	Aberdeen	2-2, 5-1
Quarter Final	Kilmarnock	4-2
Semi Final	Motherwell	3-1
Final	St. Mirren	2-0

1962-63

For the first time in thirteen years, the club retained the trophy. Jim Baxter was magnificent as Celtic were trounced 3-0 in this first 'Old Firm' final in thirty-five years. Rangers had now equalled their great rivals' 17 Scottish Cup triumphs.

Round 2	Airdrie	6-0
Round 3	East Stirlingshire	7-2
Quarter Final	Dundee	1-1, 3-2
Semi Final	Dundee United	5-2
Final	Celtic	1-1, 3-0

1963-64

One of the truly great Cup Finals saw the Ibrox men achieve victory with two goals in the last two minutes and record a 3-1 scoreline over Dundee. Ralph Brand became the first player to score in three successive Scottish Cup Finals. For a third time, the club had captured this trophy three years running. Also, there was the small matter of another 'treble'!

Round 1	Stenhousemuir	5-1
Round 2	Duns	9-0
Round 3	Partick Thistle	3-0
Quarter Final	Celtic	2-0
Semi Final	Dunfermline	1-0
Final	Dundee	3-1

1965-66

Kai Johansen's wonder strike in the replay against Celtic was the only goal of the game. The Danish internationalist became the first foreigner to win a Scottish Cup winner's medal. Understandably, he is now part of Rangers folklore.

Round 1	Airdrie	5-1
Round 2	Ross County	2-0
Quarter Final	St. Johnstone	1-0
Semi Final	Aberdeen	0-0, 2-1
Final	Celtic	0-0, 1-0

1972-73

The Centenary Cup Final was also won in dramatic fashion when Tom Forsyth's famous 'six-inch' goal secured an emotional 3-2 triumph over oldest rivals, Celtic. Derek Parlane and Alfie Conn were the other scorers. After a period with Tottenham Hotspur in London, Conn committed the ultimate sin - he signed for Celtic!

Round 3	Dundee United	1-0
Round 4	Hibernian	1-1, 2-1
Quarter Final	Airdrie	2-0
Semi Final	Ayr United	2-0
Final	Celtic	3-2

1975-76

It was felt that, after a 'semi' in which the 'Light Blues' came from 2-0 behind in the last twenty minutes to defeat Motherwell 3-2, the final itself could only be more straightforward. In fact, within one minute, Hearts were a goal down and Rangers went on to a 3-1 victory, with Derek Johnstone scoring twice.

Round 3	East Fife	3-0
Round 4	Aberdeen	4-1
Quarter Final	Queen of the South	5-0
Semi Final	Motherwell	3-2
Final	Hearts	3-1

1977-78

Although only one goal separated the teams, the Ibrox club were head and shoulders above their opponents from Aberdeen. The 2-1 scoreline failed to convey the real difference between the rivals.

Derek Johnstone scored the winner on a day when the vision and class of Bobby Russell, in midfield, was a joy to behold.

Round 3	Berwick Rangers	4-2
Round 4	Stirling Albion	1-0
Quarter Final	Kilmarnock	4-1
Semi Final	Dundee United	2-0
Final	Aberdeen	2-1

1978-79

After two goalless matches against Hibernian, the trophy was finally lifted in a second replay which Rangers won 3-2. The winner was courtesy of an extra-time own-goal by Arthur Duncan after Alex Miller had missed a penalty.

Round 3	Motherwell	3-1
Round 4	Kilmarnock	1-1, 1-0
Quarter Final	Dundee	6-3
Semi Final	Partick Thistle	0-0, 1-0
Final	Hibernian	0-0, 0-0, 3-2

1980-81

Yet another final replay. Davie Cooper, John MacDonald and Derek Johnstone were all reinstated after the initial 0-0 draw with Dundee United. A very different Rangers team (in more ways than one) were really quite superb 4-1 victors. Davie Cooper was 'simply the best'.

Round 3	Airdrie	5-0
Round 4	St. Johnstone	3-3, 3-1
Quarter Final	Hibernian	3-1
Semi Final	Morton	2-1
Final	Dundee United	0-0, 4-1

1991-92

It had been a long eleven-year wait but the trophy returned to Govan, at last, following the 2-1 defeat of Airdrie. However, it is the 'semi' that most fans still recall. This was the night when, in atrocious conditions, ten-man Rangers heroically defied a second-half Celtic onslaught. Fullback, David Robertson, was ordered off in just six minutes. Ally McCoist's goal just before the interval proved to be enough, though and a very famous victory belonged to Rangers.

Round 3	Aberdeen	1-0
Round 4	Motherwell	2-1
Quarter Final	St. Johnstone	3-0
Semi Final	Celtic	1-0
Final	Airdrie	2-1

1992-93

It was the youngest player on the park, Neil Murray, who opened the scoring. Mark Hateley added a second and that was enough, even though opponents, Aberdeen, pulled one back late on. Final score: Rangers 2, Aberdeen 1.

Round 3	Motherwell	2-0
Round 4	Ayr United	2-0
Quarter Final	Arbroath	3-0
Semi Final	Hearts	2-1
Final	Aberdeen	2-1

1995-96

Simply remembered as 'The Day Of Brian Laudrup'. The 'Great Dane' destroyed Hearts, scoring twice and setting up the other three in the unforgettable 5-1 triumph. Gordon Durie's 'hat-trick' was the first in a Scottish Cup Final since 1972 and only the third in its entire history.

Round 3	Keith	10-1
Round 4	Clyde	4-1
Quarter Final	Inverness Cal. Thistle	3-0
Semi Final	Celtic	2-1
Final	Hearts	5-1